WINNERS & LOSERS, GAMBLERS ALL

WINNERS & LOSERS, GAMBLERS ALL

Memories of Historic British Columbia

Photography by
MICHAEL BREUER
Text by
ROSEMARY NEERING

Toronto
OXFORD UNIVERSITY PRESS
1984

Acknowledgements

We would like to thank Leonard McCann and the Vancouver Maritime Museum, the New Westminster Historic Centre and Museum, the Princeton Historic Society, the British Columbia Provincial Museum, Hy's Restaurants, and the staff of these institutions, Tim Cushman, Vince Campbell, Don McIntosh, Bill Hampton, and Milton Swanson, for assistance with the photographs in this book. We would also like to thank the staff of the British Columbia Provincial Archives, the Vancouver City Archives, the Northwest Room of the Vancouver Public Library, and Dave Parker and Bob Turner of the B.C. Provincial Museum, for background and research assistance. Special thanks from the writer to her father, George Hyman, for riding herd on diction, grammar and punctuation.

All photographs in this book have been taken with LEICA cameras and LEITZ lenses of the following focal lengths: 21mm, 35mm, 50mm, 90mm, 180mm and 400mm.

Canadian Cataloguing in Publication Data

Neering, Rosemary R., 1945–
Winners and losers, gamblers all

Bibliography: p.
ISBN 0-19-540465-3

1. British Columbia—History—1871–1903—Pictorial
works.* 2. Historic building—British Columbia
Pictorial works. I. Title. II. Breuer, Michael.

FC3812.N43 1984   971.1   C84-098756-0
F1087.8′N43 1984

Produced by Roger Boulton Publishing Services
Designed by Fortunato Aglialoro

1 2 3 4 – 7 6 5 4

Printed in Hong Kong
by Scanner Art Services, Inc., Toronto

Introduction

SOME YEARS AGO, two optimistic prospectors founded a company to operate a gold mine in northern British Columbia. The mine couldn't miss: it was get-rich-quick time for the hundreds of eager investors who bought the stock. Three years later, the company had subsided, not too gracefully, into the mire of bankruptcy. Undeterred, the next time promoters came around with news of another can't-miss gold mine, many of the same investors pulled out their chequebooks, delighted to have been given a second chance.

About the same time that news of the first mine was on everyone's lips, a West Coast wheeler-dealer was increasingly in the news. Stocks, real estate, sports, even love—everything he touched turned golden. A year or two later, disaster struck: gold turned to dross, profits to losses and loan-happy bankers gave way to accountants with eyebrows raised. Even love turned to something less, as marital problems hit the headlines.

The principals in these two stories and many others like them may have thought their experiences were unique. Had they looked a little closer at British Columbia history, they might have recognized that they were just the latest players in the traditional British Columbia gambling game for winners and losers.

In British Columbia, we've never left behind the gambling spirit of the frontier. That's hardly surprising: on any time-line, British Columbia's written history looks pretty puny. After all, it's barely 200 years since the first weatherbeaten sailing ship nosed its way up the coast, its crew seeking a sea route across this nuisance of a North American continent. (The first, that is, unless you believe the stories of Juan de Fuca, who claimed he sailed this coast in 1592, and started a good B.C. tradition by recounting his experiences thereafter in every bar overlooking the Adriatic.)

Ever since that first voyage, the overriding spirit of those who have come to British Columbia has been the feeling that somewhere out there lies the opportunity to succeed, the certainty that fortune rests on the lucky cut of the cards.

From those beginnings onward, British Columbia has been about risk. The explorers who sailed the coast or sought the mountain passes were here on a bet that they could capture the rich fur-trading grounds for their country, their company or themselves. For the 'gentlemen adventurers trading out of Hudson Bay', the emphasis was more on the adventure than on the gentlemen. For them and for their competitors, it was all risk in an unknown land with an unmeasured prize at stake.

Probably no one has been more of a gambler than the prospector in the gold rush of the mid-nineteenth century. He followed the fur trader to a land that had little white settlement and no roads worthy of the name, and with absolutely no certainty of gain. Often, he was ill-prepared to survive in the wilderness. He came, not soberly to settle and farm, but with a gambler's spirit to heed the capricious call of gold.

Gold wasn't the only lure. In succeeding years, silver, copper, coal, platinum, all drew prospectors into the game. Some did win, yet many a winner lost in the end. Those who made fortunes by day often frittered them away by night, in the gambling rooms, saloons and red-light houses of the shanty mining-towns.

Vancouver historian Alan Morley records that in the early days of Vancouver (then known as Granville), a man bet $100 on which of two flies would crawl to the top of a bar mirror first. 'It is not to be wondered at,' says Morley. 'A man had to be a gambler or he wouldn't be in Granville at all. He was gambling, as a rule, his time, his own future and all his worldly possessions on the future of this hamlet in the wilderness; a trifle more bet on the location of a card or the behaviour of a housefly was neither here nor there.'†

Which is not to say that gamblers are inevitably losers. The stories of the losers are more entertaining than those of the winners, but winners there were aplenty in the land. Partners in the fur companies; owners of stores and stagecoaches; backers of mining companies, sawmills and railways: the shrewdest entrepreneurs were often the big winners in a high stakes game.

That same division between winners and losers, labourers and lords of finance, is reflected in the historic buildings of British Columbia. Most of the buildings that actually witnessed the roistering times of fur, gold and timber are gone now, marked only by the presence of a squared log in the bush or shards of china beside the faint track of a onetime road. These buildings were meant to be transitory, thrown up quickly to house and service those who might well be gone next year or next week. Fire, flood and the passage of time have destroyed many of these structures. Some few remain in ghost towns, sagging a little deeper into decay each year. Some have been herded together onto historic sites, creating a tiny warp in time that allows us to look back at life on the early frontier.

There were to be sure more solid buildings of brick and stone. Most of these stand in towns and cities still, far from the remains of mining and logging camps. Some are sturdy mansions, testimony to the financial success of their original owners. Some are public edifices, built to enclose and symbolize the powers of government and God.

Few have overwhelming architectural significance. The early days of

---

†Morley, Alan. *Vancouver, from Milltown to Metropolis*. Vancouver: Mitchell Press, 1961.

British Columbia did not lend themselves to great architecture. But we value these buildings nonetheless, for they form the one solid link with a history that has gone by so fast that its implications are hard to grasp. So much has changed in such a short time that sometimes it is difficult to see our connections with our past.

The buildings are our visible connections. With each year that passes, we seem to cherish them a little more. In the past decade there has been a surge of interest in historic sites; heritage associations have been formed, grants provided for restorations, bylaws passed to preserve old buildings, whole areas renovated to ensure that they will survive without change of style.

British Columbia is still a province that sags and soars with the highs and lows of the markets. British Columbians are still people who react to the swings with elation or dismay. Our historic buildings—and the stories of the winners and losers behind them—serve to remind us that the gambling game we and the province play is a long-lived part of the British Columbia tradition.

ROSEMARY NEERING

BIBLIOGRAPHY

Books:

Cook, James. *Captain Cook's Voyages around the World.* Newcastle: M. Brown, 1790.

Fraser, Simon. (W.K. Lamb, ed.) *The Letters and Journals of Simon Fraser 1806–1808.* Toronto: Macmillan, 1960.

Howay, F.W., and Scholefield, E.O.S. *British Columbia from the Earliest Times to the Present.* Vancouver: The S.J. Clarke Publishing Company, 1914.

Large, R.G. *Skeena: River of Destiny.* Vancouver: Mitchell Press, 1957.

Leonoff, C.E. *Pioneers, Pedlars and Prayer Shawls.* Vancouver: Sono Nis, 1978.

McDonald, Archibald. *Peace River: A Canoe Voyage from Hudson's Bay to the Pacific, by the late Sir George Simpson.* Ottawa: J. Durie, 1872.

Macfie, Matthew. *Vancouver Island and British Columbia.* London: Longman, Green, Longman, Roberts and Green, 1865.

McKelvie, B.A. *Fort Langley: Outpost of Empire.* Vancouver: Vancouver Daily Province, 1947.

Milton, Viscount William F., and Cheadle, W.B. *The North-West Passage by Land.* London: Cassell, Petter and Galpin, 1865.

Morice, A.G. *The History of the Northern Interior of British Columbia.* Toronto: W. Briggs, 1904.

Morley, Alan. *Vancouver, from Milltown to Metropolis.* Vancouver: Mitchell Press, 1961.

Phillips, Paul. *No Power Greater: a Century of Labor in British Columbia.* Vancouver: British Columbia Federation of Labour, 1967.

Steele, Sir Samuel B. *Forty Years in Canada.* New York: Dodd, Mead, 1915.

Veillette, John, and White, Gary. *Early Indian Village Churches.* Vancouver: University of British Columbia Press, 1977.

Work, John (Henry Drummond Dee, ed.) *The Journal of John Work.* Victoria: C.F. Banfield, 1945.

Pamphlets, Articles, Manuscripts:

Anderson, James. 'Sawney's Letters and Cariboo Rhymes.' Barkerville: *Cariboo Sentinel,* 1869.

British Columbia Department of Agriculture. 'Annual Report.' Victoria: Queen's Printer, 1900.

Canadian Pacific Railway. 'Facts for Farmers.' Liverpool: Canadian Pacific Railway, 1887.

Melrose, Robert. 'The Diary of Robert Melrose.' *British Columbia Historical Quarterly,* 1943.

Parish Register, St. John the Divine, Hammond.

NORTH PACIFIC COAST—'We were reduced to two courses and close reefed topsails, having a very hard gale with rain right on shore; so that instead of running in for the land I was glad to get an offing. . . . Sometimes in an evening, the wind would moderate and veer to the Southward, this was always a sure prelude to a Storm, which blew the hardest at SSE and was attended with rain and Sleet. It seldom lasted above four or six hours, before it was succeeded by another gale from the NW which generally brought with it fair weather; it was only by the means of these southerly blasts that we got to the NW at all.' The words are those of Captain James Cook, standing offshore and seeking landfall north of the 49th parallel late in March of 1778. He spoke for many a mariner before and after that date, for landing on the coast of the future British Columbia was not a simple matter. Those on board the Spanish ship *Santiago* in 1774 were the first to catch glimpses of the coast, but storm, fog and wind drove them away. Cook did set foot on land, at Nootka Cove, and thus the men of his expedition became the first Europeans to touch what would be British Columbian soil.

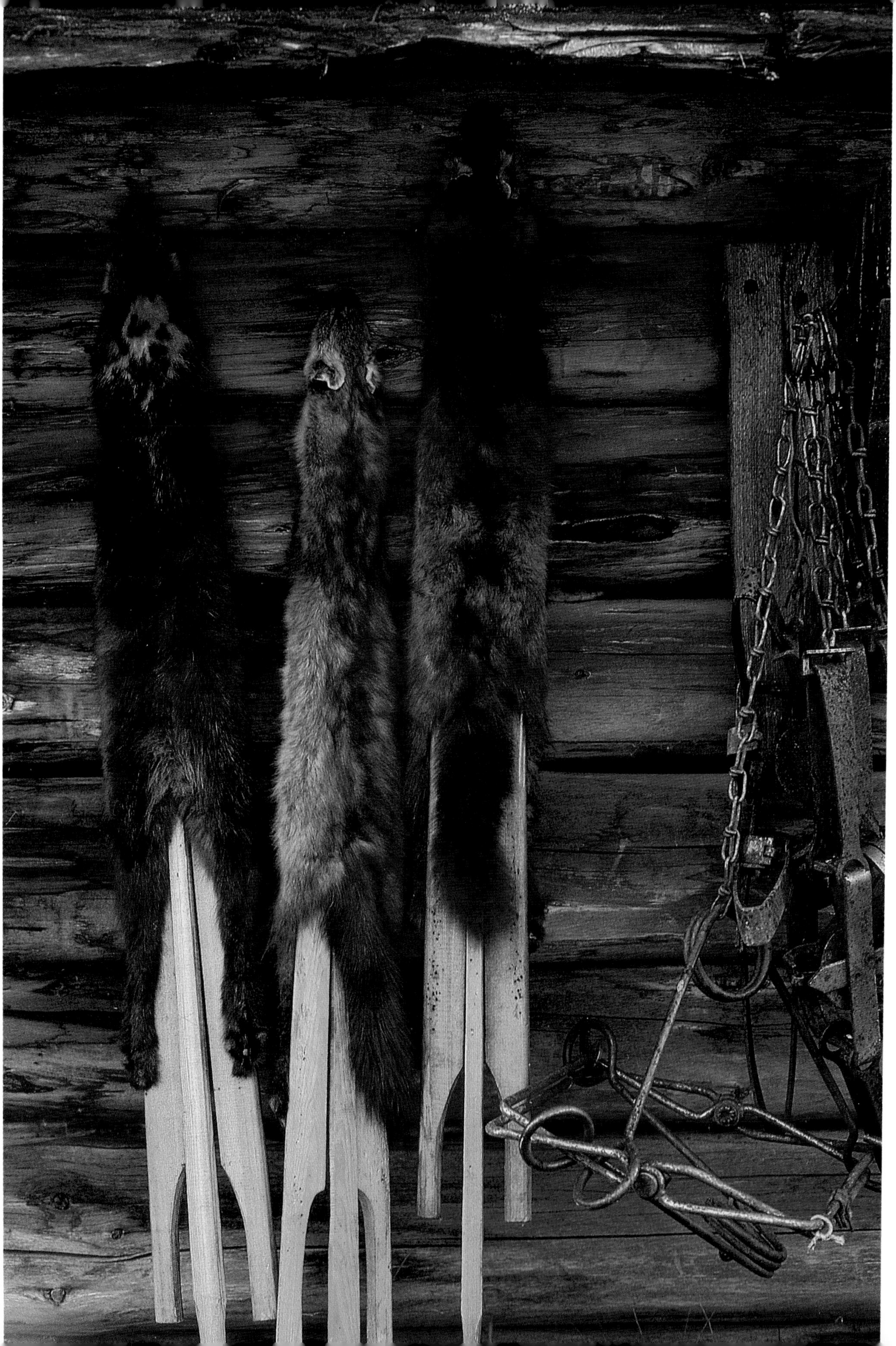

CAPTAIN VANCOUVER'S CHRONOMETER, MARITIME MUSEUM, VANCOUVER—Was there a passage by sea to the Orient? Did this unwieldy continent of North America completely block the direct way west from Europe to Asia? The question continued to plague and fascinate seamen to the end of the eighteenth century. Early explorers who came to test the coasts of this nuisance continent had their task made more difficult by the fact that they could not be sure exactly where they were. In 1714, the British Admiralty offered a prize of 20,000 pounds sterling to anyone who could devise a reliable way of measuring longitude at sea. The prize went unclaimed. In fact, the invention of the chronometer, a seagoing timepiece that did make it possible to measure longitude, did not receive the prize. It did change forever the ways of the mapmakers. James Cook took one of the new inventions with him on his second and third voyages, in 1771 and 1777-8. Captain George Vancouver charted the British Columbia coast with the aid of this Arnold 176 50-hour Expedition Marine Chronometer, completed in 1791 for the British Board of Longitude. Vancouver had already sailed by the time the chronometer was ready; it was sent to him at Nootka on board a supply ship. After the voyages of Vancouver, the chronometer was returned to storage in 1795, sent to Australia briefly in 1801, and returned home on a whaler; it then disappeared until its discovery in a private collection in 1981. Auctioned at Christie's in London, it was bought by the Vancouver Maritime Museum, where it is now on display.

FURS AND TRAPS, CARIBOO TRAPLINE (*left*) The fashions of other continents dictated the winners and losers in the fur trade, British Columbia's first great gambling game. Sea-otter furs from the coast could be sold at a handsome price in the courts of China. Beaver pelts from the land were headed for Europe, where the soft inner hair was transformed into felt for men's hats. Explorers from rival fur companies sought trade routes to the sea, sites for fur posts and all the rich peltry they felt sure would be available in this territory of New Caledonia. Russians, Spaniards, Americans, British, and those who felt loyalty to no country, all competed for furs along the coast. The best years were early in the nineteenth century, yet by 1835 trader John Work could still report a handsome bounty from a trading trip: '38 sea otters, 717 beavers, 9 land otters, 31 bears, 46 martens, 38 minks and some other small furs, which is certainly far beyond what I expected.' So many furs were obtained by the traders on the ship *Lama* that they and Work ran out of the blankets that were the Hudson's Bay Company main items of trade. Instead of the usual blanket and '2 gall. mixed rum' per beaver pelt, they began trading such items as a 'swivil gun', a metal scabbard sabre, a cask of molasses, a cask of rice, a shirt, vest and trousers, and '20 yd. fine calico and 2 gall. mixed rum for a bear.'

FORT ST. JAMES—'At the last lake,' wrote Chief Factor Archibald McDonald of a trip to Fort St. James in 1828, 'within a mile of the fort, we halted for breakfast and changed. The day as yet being fine, the flag was put up; the piper in fine Highland costume, and every arrangement was made to arrive at Fort St. James in the most imposing manner we could, for the sake of the Indians. Accordingly, a gun was fired, the bugle sounded, and soon after the piper commenced the celebrated march of the clans, *si coma leum cagadh na shea*— Peace; or war if you will it otherwise.' A dignified procession to impress the residents of this far outpost of empire. Fort St. James was founded by Simon Fraser in 1806; it is the oldest continuously inhabited white settlement in the province. Its business was fur trading, first as a fort of the Northwest Company, then of the Hudson's Bay Company after the two merged in 1821. Each year, some 100 packs of furs, mostly beaver and marten, were taken out by the fur brigade. Isolated by distance and terrain, Fort St. James had few of the creature comforts of forts located closer to major transportation routes. The buying of furs and the eating of salmon—fresh, dried, salted, cured—were the only activities that could be counted upon to occur with any regularity.

FORT LANGLEY—30 July 1827, diary of James McMillan, leader of an expedition of men of the Hudson's Bay Company: 'The schooner was brought close to the shore, and the horses landed by slinging them off to the bank. The poor animals seemed to rejoice heartily in their liberation. Our men at noon were all busily employed clearing the ground for the establishment. . . . One of the ship's crew was this day put in irons for making use of language calculated to promote discontent and create disorder among the crew.' The building of the new company post on the Fraser River was underway. French Canadians, Sandwich Islanders, Americans, Scots, English and Indians set to work. By 14 August the first bastion was complete. By 8 September the square was enclosed and the gate hung. And by New Year's Day 1828 the men had settled in. On that day they visited the officers' quarters, to receive a glass of wine, a piece of cake, a little flour, some dried peas—and, more to the point, a large piece of venison and a pint of rum each. Fort Langley existed on this site for 11 years, years marked by the beginning of farming, the setting up of a salmon industry, the passage of the yearly fur brigade, and occasional alarums and excursions caused by altercations with local Indians.

SALMON BARRELS, FORT LANGLEY—The men of the Hudson's Bay Company soon took advantage of the resources of the Fraser River. Chief Trader Archie McDonald quickly calculated that the salmon he had obtained from the Indians in trade had cost the company just a halfpenny each. If fish such as these could be cured, barrelled and shipped out, there would be a good profit for the Company. He experimented, and wrote to Governor Simpson of the results: 'We were fortunate to procure upwards of 15,000 (fish); enough to make up more than 200 Barrels...However, I fear...the first Cargo will not stand the Test of a foreign market, and trust by the next Season, we shall be provided with a good Cooper, that will know something of fish curing.' McDonald was correct; the barrels were poorly made and the fish went bad. But coopers were sent, better barrels were made and an industry was established. White pine was found at the mouth of a river that flowed into the Fraser (named the Stave River on account of its timber) and by the early 1830's cured and casked fish was being regularly shipped from the fort to points abroad.

FORT LANGLEY—By the late 1830's, the shortcomings of Fort Langley's site were evident. The main problem was the distance between the fort and the farmlands that seemed best for the Company's purposes. In 1839 work began on a new fort a few miles from the old one. Within a very short time the new fort was established and the old was abandoned. Then, one April night in 1840, flames flared forth from the blacksmith's shop, occupied, appropriately at the time, by a man named Brulé. In scarcely more than minutes the fort was destroyed. The new fort rose quickly on the same site; it is the one which now stands, restored, on the banks of the Fraser. The glory years of the fur trade were almost over by the time this fort was built. Changing fashions in Europe saw the beaver hat abandoned and the derby and Italian silk topper take its place. Floods, cold winters, and a decline in the number of furs traded in the interior, also plagued the fort. Gold, not furs, brought a rebirth in 1859, but the activity at the fort was soon transferred to Fort Yale and other waypoints to Cariboo. Fort Langley did have its moments of importance. It is generally regarded as the birthplace of British Columbia, for it was here on 19 November 1859 that a solemn ceremony took place officially establishing B.C. as a separate colonial entity.

FORT ST. JAMES—Isolated they might be, but the Hudson's Bay Company men posted to New Caledonia were not to forget that they represented an enterprise chartered as 'gentlemen adventurers'. Father A.G. Morice, Oblate missionary at Stuart Lake and pioneer historian notes, 'The gentlemen were as well provided...as the extreme difficulties of the communications would allow. Even such luxuries as Madeira and port wines appeared at their mess.' There was, of course, a class difference. 'Dried salmon and cold water took the place of all this in the servants' quarters.' It is recorded, even, that some men died of the effects of too much salmon. Each person who worked for the Hudson's Bay Company had a clearly

defined place on the scale. The indentured servants formed the lower class. Next came the clerks, who did the clerical work, engaged in trade and might aspire to run a post. They sat in the officers' mess, slept in the officers' quarters, were called 'gentlemen', and were addressed as 'Mr.' in correspondence. Above them, and beyond even their aspirations, were the commissioned gentlemen, who were partners in the company. These men, chief factors and chief traders, were accorded the ultimate accolade: they had 'Esquire' appended to their names. And it wouldn't do to let appearances slide. Two silk-hat-covers are included in a list of possessions enumerated at Fort St. James in 1836.

CRAIGFLOWER MANOR—The standard English manor farm of the nineteenth century was a world unto itself, orderly and self-sufficient. That was the model that the Hudson's Bay Company envisioned near Fort Victoria on Vancouver Island, to provide farm produce for the fort and for trade with the Russians who worked the north coast. Craigflower was one of four farms, and the only one that came up to manor farm standards. Kenneth Mackenzie came from England to run the farm; by 1854 he had built a stately manor house, a sawmill, a grist mill, a bakery, lime kilns, a slaughterhouse, a ship chandlery and a general store. Compare this to the progress of Captain Edward Langford, who ran Colwood Farm; one year he charged the Company an amount eight times his annual salary for goods used to provide entertainments for himself and his family and friends. Craigflower, on the other hand, supplied its own needs and those of its customers; the Royal Navy took on one order 9230 pounds of biscuit and 4392 of bread. But not everyone was happy in the well-ordered world of Craigflower. The labourers imported to work the farm sometimes lost heart. 'The change from the cottage homes and fertile fields of East Lothian to the dense and primeval forest of Vancouver Island was so great,' wrote James Deans, 'that sometimes I used to wander out in the bush and sit down, give vent to my grief in a flood of tears.'

CRAIGFLOWER SCHOOL—It wasn't a spelling bee that brought Craigflower School its first publicity; it was a building bee, held in 1854, to erect the school frame. A contemporary chronicler, whose main concern seems to have been to record the degree of intoxication of the populace at any given time, reported, 'whole company in general notoriously drunk.' But the work did go on and by March of the following year eight boys and six girls were enrolled for the study of reading, writing, arithmetic, geography, grammar, natural history, and spiritual subjects. Craigflower School was built of lumber milled and bricks cast at Craigflower Farm and boated across the narrow inlet to the school site. Now the oldest standing schoolhouse west of the Great Lakes, Craigflower served as a school for 56 years. Twenty years after it closed as a school it was reopened as a museum.

FRASER CANYON (*right*)—The scenic wonders of beautiful British Columbia impressed the early explorers not at all. They would have happily traded the rushing rivers for wide streams that required no portages, and the picturesque, snow-capped peaks for some good flat prairie. One of the most difficult stretches for travel was the Fraser Canyon. Simon Fraser, whose name was given to the river, was emphatic: 'I have never seen anything to equal this country, for I cannot find words to describe our situation at times. We had to pass where no human being should venture.' Still, the Fraser provided the most convenient route for a passage from the mountains to the sea, and when the time came for roads and railways, engineers and navvies followed Fraser's footsteps, not his warning.

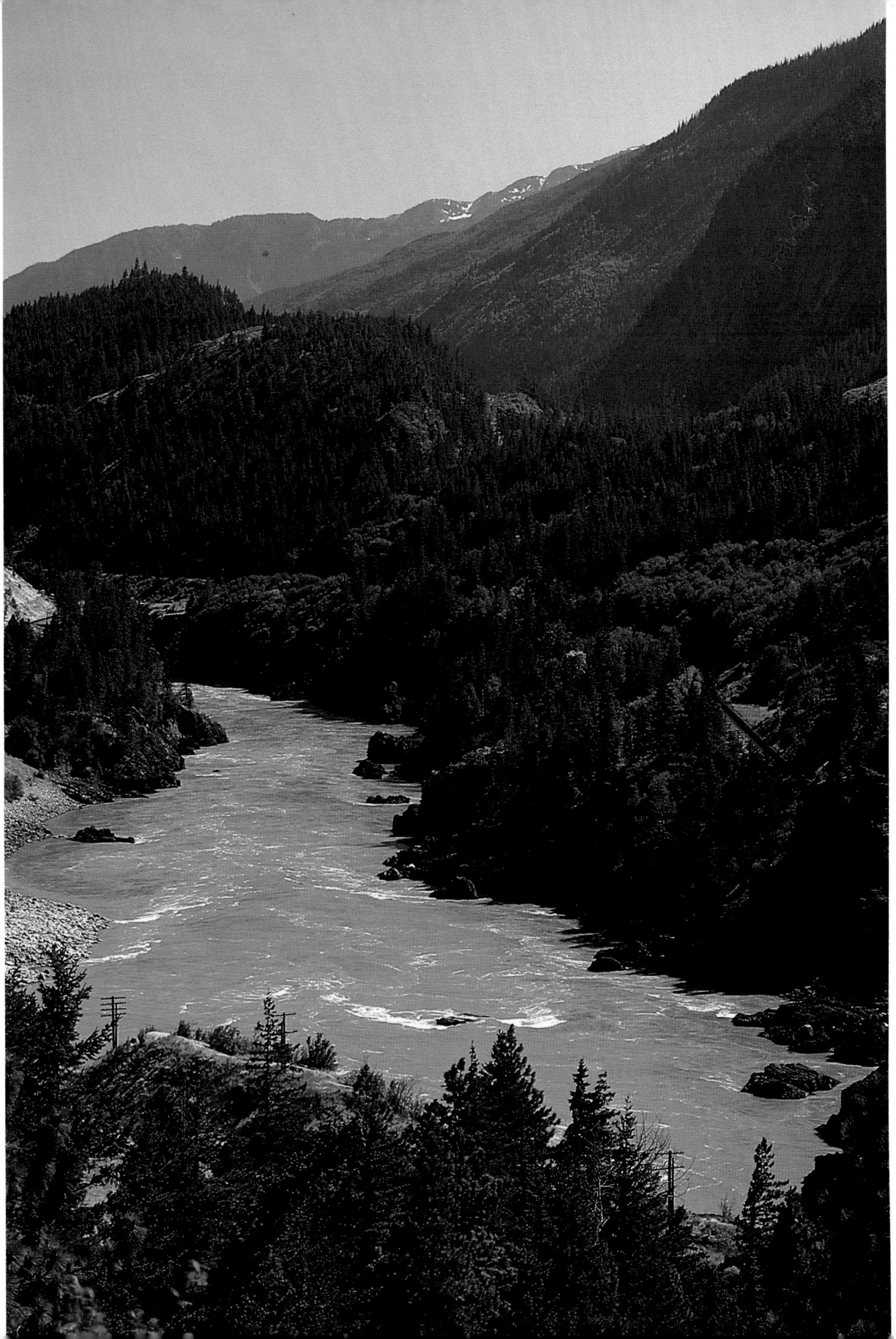

FOOL'S GOLD: IRON PYRITES FROM THE CARIBOO—It could be said that all gold is fool's gold: fools those who chase it and fools those who believe its promises. The men who struggled to make their fortunes in the Cariboo gold rush must sometimes have questioned the fruits of their labour. For every man who struck it rich, another hundred stayed poor. Even the luckiest ran out of luck. Both Dutch Bill Dietz, whose find on Williams Creek started the rush north in earnest, and Billy Barker, who found the richest vein of all, died in poverty, their money leached away by drink and gambling and hangers-on. Yet the rush that destroyed some men and their dreams built the foundations of British Columbia. The ranchers, storekeepers, bankers and settlers stayed on after the gold fever cooled. The arrival of the gold rushers brought the declaration of British Columbia as a separate colony. It also brought the building of the Cariboo Road to the interior, and the institutions of law and of formal government to the mainland.

GOLD PANNER ON THE FRASER RIVER—The first gold showed its glitter in the sandbars of the rivers and creeks. The gold seekers flocked in by the hundreds, then the thousands, turning Victoria into a tent town and Fort Langley into chaos. Their target was the bars of the Fraser River; the silt carried downriver to form the bars was dug and washed and swirled until gold glimmered from the bottom of the goldpan. Not for everyone, though—the early arrivals denounced the Fraser as the great humbug when spring floods completely covered the bars. Those who stayed until the water subsided found enough gold to bring a new surge of prospectors the next year. Every likely-looking creek from Yale to Cariboo was sampled and sampled again. Many yielded pay dirt. And when the gold pan was not in use for seeking colours, it came in handy as a frying pan, a bread oven or as a washpan for socks.

CARIBOO ROAD, NEAR HOPE—Gold has the nasty habit of occurring in places difficult of access, and Cariboo gold was no exception. Each of the three possible routes from coast to Cariboo had its drawbacks. The route through the Oregon Territory overland to the Okanagan was blocked by wars between American troops and Indians. Governor James Douglas hired miners down on their luck to build a road on the second route, from the head of Harrison Lake. But this was little more than a rough trail, and was difficult and unpopular. The third way lay beside the Fraser River. To Yale, the matter was simple; steamboats could ascend to here, the lower end of the Fraser Canyon. In 1861 Douglas launched the project that would be one of the major achievements of his governorship, the building of a one-and-a-half metre wide coach road from Yale to Barkerville. A company of Royal Engineers dispatched to the colony to bolster the British presence surveyed and built the most difficult part of the road, through the canyon. Some sections were blasted out of sheer cliffs; others hung out over the river on stilts and cribbing. Private contractors slogged through mud and rock to build the rest. The 650 kilometres of road were complete by 1865. Along the road passed loaded wagons, stagecoaches, swift horses and slower pack-mules, herds of cattle, settlers, gamblers—and even camels. Only the camels were not a success. They terrified the other animals with their smell, cut their tender feet on the sharp rocks and earned themselves a reputation for orneriness. In the end, they were released across the Fraser; the last survivor was reported to have died early in this century.

IRVING HOUSE, NEW WESTMINSTER—Captain William Irving wasn't the type to settle for a rough log-house in the wilderness. Irving, owner of British Columbia's first steamship fleet, had his house designed by Royal Engineers and precut red cedar shipped from California to create a residence worthy of his family and his position. Irving hired a disbanded engineers' company to build his house with care and precision. It included a drawing-room seven and a half by six metres, and was graced by marble fireplaces imported from England and a mahogany staircase shipped from Scotland. After the shell was built, the house was left to settle for a year before a plaster skin was applied. In the house, as in business, Irving would not settle for less than he wanted. A Scotsman who arrived in British Columbia in 1858, Irving put the sternwheeler *Governor Douglas* on the Victoria-Hope run soon after the start of the gold rush. Within a few years, he had established a fleet that later became the nucleus of the Canadian Pacific Steamships coastal service. His most startling experience took place not on one of his own boats but on a competitor's. In those days, there was a strong rivalry for the speed championship on the Fraser run, a rivalry that frequently caused the sternwheeler captains to build the steam pressure high—on this occasion too high. The boiler blew, hurling passengers and crew overboard and killing eight. Irving was lucky; he landed, unharmed, on a sandbank.

16

POINT ELLICE HOUSE, VICTORIA—A gracious house on the Selkirk waters was the home of Peter and Caroline Agnes Trutch O'Reilly. O'Reilly was gold commissioner at the Cariboo, Columbia, Kootenay and Omineca in turn as gold fever flared and died around the territory. His wife was a member of one of British Columbia's pioneer fami-

lies and sister to a man who helped hammer out the terms of British Columbia's entry into Confederation and who became the province's first lieutenant-governor. Mrs. O'Reilly herself was a spirited lady in the tradition of the British Empire. Before her arrival in B.C., where she met and married O'Reilly, she had travelled widely, riding a camel to the Red Sea and coolly continuing the social round in India with her sisters in the middle of the Madras mutiny. Point Ellice House was built about 1861 and purchased by the O'Reillys in 1863. Thereupon Mrs. O'Reilly settled into become one of the city's better-known hostesses, inviting the city's social cream to garden parties and formal dinners. The O'Reilly's were one of three Victoria couples to entertain Sir John A. Macdonald on his 1867 visit to Victoria. Not that Mrs. O'Reilly entirely gave up travelling to devote herself to harp-playing and hospitality. She often visited the interior with her husband, and was the first to drive across the Alexandra suspension bridge, in the Fraser Canyon, a spectacular work of engineering undertaken by her brothers.

BROOM FLOWERS, NEAR VICTORIA (*right*) Anyone seeing the spreading splashes of yellow on southern Vancouver Island each spring could be forgiven for thinking that broom is native to the island. In fact, the first seeds of this sturdy Scottish plant were brought here by a settler who wanted to remind himself of his native country hills. Walter Colquhoun Grant was a captain in the Scots Greys when a bank failed and the Grant family fortune was lost. He took the honourable course; he resigned his commission and set out for the colonies, taking with him to Vancouver Island eight men, his cricket bat and a stately carriage—only to discover there were no roads in the infant colony. But there was adventure; out for a stroll near Fort Victoria one evening, he was attacked by a herd of dastardly buffalo. He blanched, but bravely drew his

trusty pistol and shot the ringleader between the eyes. Later that night, he was confronted by an angry Hudson's Bay Company herdsman, bemoaning the loss of his best milk cow. (Life was like that for the new settler.) Grant failed at farming, failed at surveying, failed at setting up a sawmill. He tried, and failed, to set up commerce between Victoria Island and the Sandwich Islands. He did bring back from a trip to these islands some broom seeds given to him by the British Consul (how broom got to Hawaii is another story). Grant sold his land and left the island before the broom took hold, before he could know that the transplanting was by far his most successful endeavour. He went back to soldiering, fought with honour in the Crimean War, and died of dysentery in India.

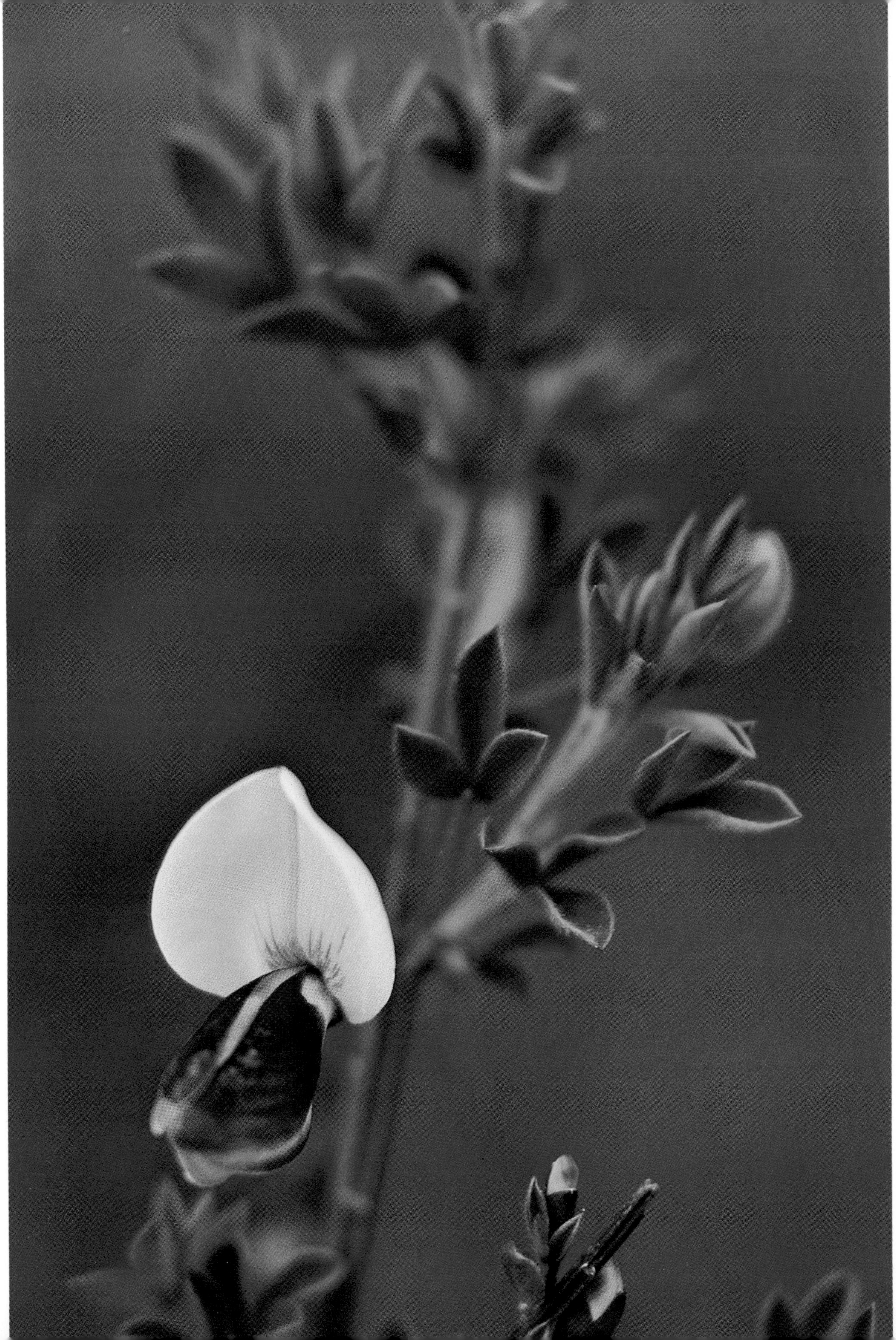

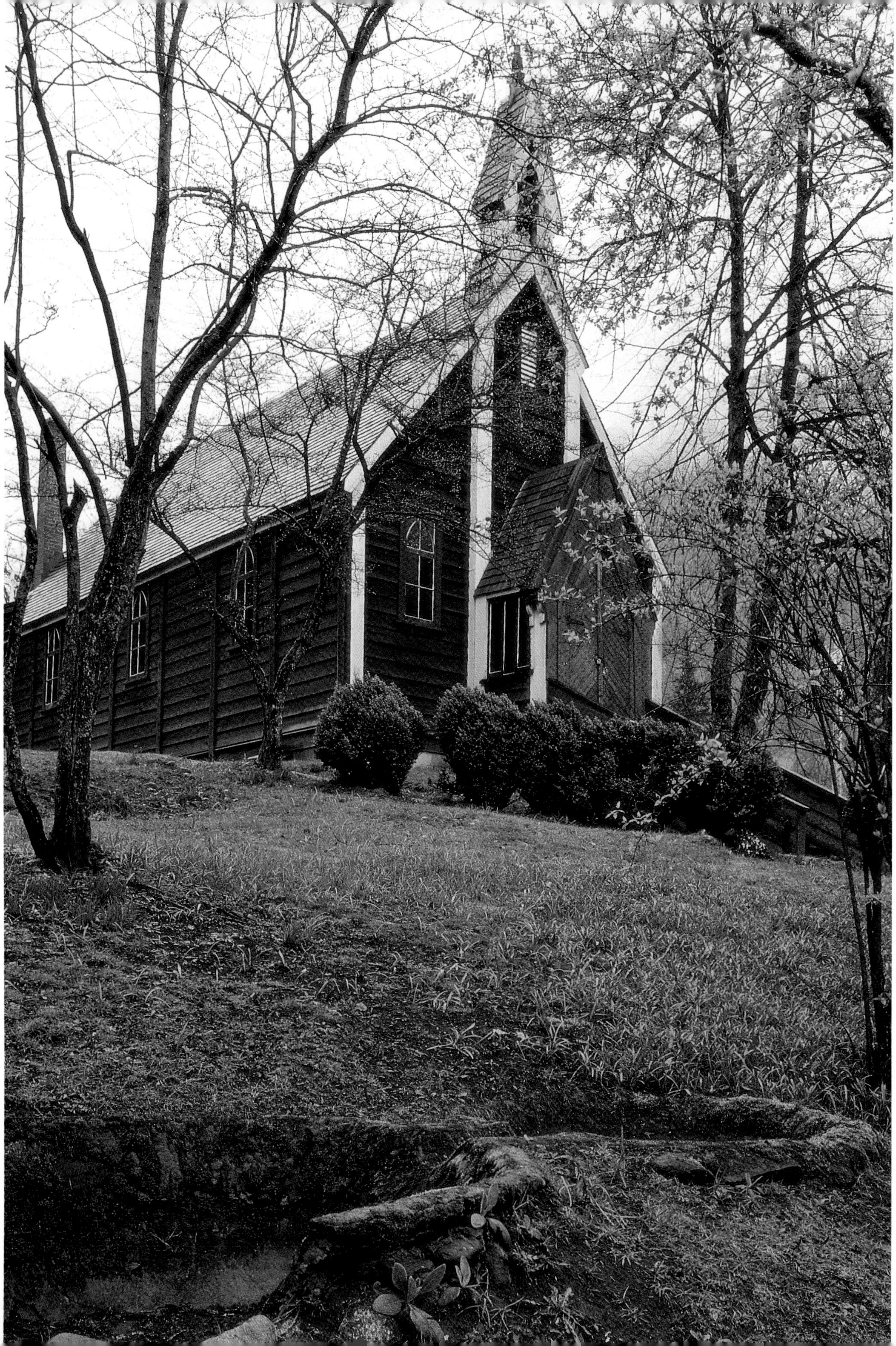

ST. JOHN THE DIVINE, DERBY AND HAMMOND—
Where the men of commerce ventured, the men of God
were not far behind. Missionaries and priests followed the
traders, to establish missions and parishes wherever they
could. St. John the Divine was one of the earliest churches
built on the British Columbia mainland. Quoth the Rev.
William Crickmer in his diary, 'The first sod was turned in
this new part of Christ's vineyard of British Columbia,
February 20th, 1859.' Crickmer's own child was the first
baptised. He notes that morning service at the church
usually brought in about six people, while afternoon
service on the spit below Fort Langley attracted between
six and forty. This part of the vineyard did not produce.
The townsite of Derby, at the old Fort Langley site, was
originally intended as the capital of British Columbia.
Then those in charge changed their minds, and the settlers
did not arrive. By 1860 Crickmer was petitioning the
Bishop for a new parish on account of the 'continued
decadence' of the old. Crickmer was sent to establish a
new church at Yale, where he soon encountered a new
type of decadence. The Derby church was moved some 20
years later, across the Fraser to a site at Hammond, where
there was a growing population of farmers and artisans.
Once again, marriages, deaths, births, and baptisms are
recorded in the church register. The register tells its own
story of the difficulties of these early settlers; of 65 deaths
listed in the first few years, 13 were those of infants.

ST. JOHN THE DIVINE, YALE (*left*) The Rev. Crickmer
got his wish for a busier parish, one with a good deal more
work for him to do. Yale came to life with the gold rush; at
the head of navigation on the Fraser River, it was the
staging point for those leaving the river steamers and
looking for land transportation to take them north. St.
John the Divine was built by Royal Engineers in 1860, just
a block from the bustling Front Street saloons. Crickmer
was happy with his new location: 'The bishop made his
appearance,' he records, 'and we opened our unpretending
little church. I had gone round and obtained funds by
subscription to buy an harmonium which after much
delay arrived from Victoria just in time for our service.'

That done, the Reverend took the measure of his competition. After considerable argument, he managed to per-
suade the Front Street businesses to close down during
Sunday service; he records that his ringing of a bell was
followed by the sound of doors slamming all along the
street. Although the parish was not promising ground, St.
John's received the bounty of at least one distinguished
visitor. In 1861, Lady Franklin passed through Yale, on
the expedition she mounted to seek news of her husband,
who had disappeared on his northern trip. She put mem-
bers of the expedition to work in the church, making pews
and choir stalls.

20 MAIN STREET, BARKERVILLE—Billy Barker was his name, and for him as for the others headed north that summer of 1862, gold had sounded its siren call. The gold that could be panned or washed from sandbar and stream had been exhausted. Miners now were sinking shafts deep into the rock and gravel near Williams Creek in the Cariboo. All the best claims had been staked by the time Cornish Billy and his six pals reached the creek; they staked below the canyon and were laughed at for their efforts, for there was no gold to be found there. They persevered. They dug 15 metres through gravel and past boulders. Here, they struck the richest gold deposits found in all that summer and perhaps ever in all of Cariboo. As around every successful claim, a town grew up. Barkerville became the busiest gold-rush town of all, the termi-

nus of the Cariboo Road, with houses, hotels, saloons, restaurants, a theatre, a Masonic Hall, a Chinatown, bathhouses, barbershops, laundries, any service or edifice a miner might need. Since its founding, the town has had three lives. The first was the liveliest. Cattle drives and ox trains rumbled down the main street, churning it to mire. Gold dust poured onto saloon tables and men flung the hurdy-gurdy girls so high their toes might touch the ceiling. In winter, snow buried the streets and buildings. Wise or lucky men fled to Victoria; the losers huddled around their wood stoves and looked ahead to a more fortunate season. Barkerville burned to the ground in 1868, but in less than a month had been rebuilt. In time, though, the remaining gold could be obtained only by the big companies and their hydraulic processes. The prospec-

tors and the gamblers moved on, to other gold rushes and other dreams. Barkerville became a quiet, backwoods Cariboo town. It came alive again in the 1930's Depression, when rumour had it that the price of gold was soon to rise. Prospectors, wanderers and speculators headed down the Cariboo trails once more, and Barkerville again saw bright lights and all-night parties. That rush ended as the other had. Barkerville might have shared the fate of other gold towns, abandoned and weathered back into the bush. Then, in the 1960's, the Provincial Government declared Barkerville a historic site and restored it to its appearance after the fire of 1868. These days, thousands of tourists pour through the streets each summer, trying to recapture a little of the excitement that electrified the air that day in 1862 when Billy Barker struck it rich.

STANLEY CEMETERY (*left*) The most final line between winners and losers was drawn by death, which for many in the gold rush came early and accidentally. Gravestones in the Barkerville and nearby Stanley cemeteries make grim reading. Many list the cause and age of death—at 37, from a mine cave-in; at 43, in a snowslide from a shaft-house roof; at 21, in childbirth, the child dying 10 days later; at 32, falling on an axe; at 23, falling down a mineshaft; at 32, a suicide; at 36, from gumboot gout. Others die from avalanches, exhaustion, inflammation of the bowel, in a fight—old age seems to have been the rarest cause of death. Robert Pritchard, buried in the Stanley cemetery, was luckier than most. One of 26 Welsh Adventurers who came to Barkerville in 1863, Pritchard survived the gold rush and lived for many years thereafter, dying a natural death in 1915. Others in the group, all known by number since there were nine Joneses in the party, died from such causes as being hit by a falling tree, drowning and a coal mine accident. Luck did not live with the Adventurers; few saw gold at all and few stayed in the Cariboo for more than a year or two.

QUESNELLE FORKS—Once the largest town on the mainland, Quesnelle Forks was another child of the gold rush. In 1860, it had more than 20 houses, 12 stores, a boarding house, whiskey shops and a forest of tents. The following year, it gained a government office and a jail and four women arrived in town. Twenty Chinese miners died in 1866 in a fire that destroyed Quesnelle Forks. It was rebuilt, but soon deserted by all but the Chinese miners. Forbidden by law to stake claims, these Chinese worked the claims abandoned by others, taking out enough gold to cause some chagrin to the less industrious, more fickle whites who had left the area. In the 1890's, when a new strike led to a short-lived boom, some Chinese even worked the river bottom from rafts anchored in the stream. Quesnelle Forks has suffered badly since the last Chinese settlers left in the 1920's. Grave robbers and bottle diggers have left their marks; someone even used a chain saw to remove Chinese carvings from the roof of the town's hotel.

24 STAGECOACH, COTTONWOOD HOUSE—Wheel team, swing team, lead team, two- or four- or six-horse stage, the coaches owned the road to Cariboo. Gold travelled from mine to city in the driver's treasure box, carefully secured; passengers mounted high on the box and wrapped themselves in blankets against the dawn chill; the mail bags contained eagerly-awaited news from the outside. Barnard's Express—the BX—was the famous line; it dominated stagecoach traffic on the Cariboo Road. The day's journey could begin in the dark at 3 or 4 a.m. and end at 6 p.m. when passengers and driver dismounted for a meal and a night's sleep. Up the next morning early again, and on to Cariboo with fresh horses drawing the stage on its way. Sometimes the stage would travel all night, with breaks only for meals or a fresh team. The driver was known as the whip, though the whip itself was usually used more for startling sound effects than to inflict pain. The fame of the best and the worst of the whips was widespread. Walter Cheadle, traveller, writer and raconteur, describes one of the not-so-good: '(He) was a most unquiet spirit, always engaged in talking to us or the horses, chewing, spitting, smoking and drinking, and at the last he was especially great.' On the whole though, the whips were a skilful lot, taking pride in their records for speed and safety.

HAT CREEK HOUSE (*right*) They were rough and ready dwellings, these roadhouses on the way to Cariboo, and they served a rough and ready crowd. 'Slept on the floor of the 70-Mile House,' wrote traveller Matthew Macfie, 'might be compared to a robber's cave. The floor covered with blanketed bodies. On the counter sleeps the barkeeper, to guard the liquors from any traveller that might, in a fit of thirst, so far forget himself as to get up in the night, put forth his hand without permission, and moisten his throat. My neck and hands all over mosquito bites.' Many of the roadhouses provided only communal lodgings and the shabbiest of stables with the most swaybacked of horses. Hat Creek House was of a slightly later vintage and a definitely better style. It was built in 1866, in a form known as 'Red River frame'. The side facing the road was covered in clapboard, while the others were of bare logs. It served as a hotel off and on until 1910, when it became a private dwelling. For six years, though not open as a roadhouse, it was owned by Stephen Tingley, best known of the Cariboo stagecoach whips. Tingley was whip, partner, director, then sole owner of the BX between 1864 and 1897. He drove a six-horse stage for 28 years without a single accident, and claimed the record for the fastest trip from Cariboo to Yale, taking a prisoner and his guards over the 600 kilometres in 30 hours.

ST. SAVIOUR'S CHURCH, BARKERVILLE—St. Saviour's must have seemed out of place in the early days of Barkerville, for salvation was the farthest thing from a miner's mind in those roistering times. That was the hard lesson learned by the Reverend James Reynard, who arrived in Barkerville in 1868. He was determined to build a church but his first winter was a record of futility; the saloon he commandeered to use as a house of worship was burned in the fire of 1868, and with it went all his possessions. There was little money to sustain him and none at all to build a church. 'We live as cheaply as possible,' he recorded, 'potatoes on Sundays by way of marking the Christian feast and cabbage at Christmas as a very special luxury. We tried more stringent measures than these, but I was losing my memory and getting morbidly afraid of meeting people.' In time, though, he found funds. St. Saviour's opened in the September, giving the miners a chance to prove that 'men working underground still have hopes that go upward and heavenward.' Reynard's church proved far sturdier than its builder. St. Saviour's still stands. Ill health forced Reynard back to Vancouver Island in 1871 and he died in 1875, worn out by his Barkerville days.

NIGHT-LIFE IN BARKERVILLE—Gambling and drinking and dance-hall girls were closer to the heart of many a miner than any Sunday sermon. In 1867, there were 12 saloons and two breweries in Barkerville, along with who knows how many stills, and houses that a minister would rather not enter. Barkerville poet James Anderson summed up the gamblers thus: 'There is a set o' men up here/ Wha' never work thro' a' the year,/ A kind o' serpent, crawlin' snakes/ That fleece the miner o' his stakes/ . . .I ne'er met/ An honest man a gambler yet.' Yet drinking and gambling and wenching still left the prospec-

tor a little time for compassion. They wouldn't all go to hear the Rev. Reynard preach on Sunday mornings, but they felt someone should attend. One group of miners, so the story goes, cut the cards each Saturday night during their regular poker game. Low man was deputized to represent the rest at Sunday service. The same storyteller says that, when he cut the low card, the church was never so full as the next morning, when half the town sidled in for the joy of seeing the greatest reprobate in town sitting, starched and polished, in the front pew.

ASHCROFT MANOR—'Tally-ho' to the hounds, and after the brute—but the brute was a coyote, the hounds were imported and the dells and creeks of England were replaced by the sagebrush and sand of the Ashcroft area. Clement Francis Cornwall and Henry Rennant Cornwall opened their Ashcroft Manor roadhouse in 1863, just in time for the first heavy traffic along the newly completed Cariboo road. Within a year or two, the brothers had erected a waterwheel, and had in operation a sawmill and a grist mill that protected them from the high price of flour brought in along the road. Their inn was popular, acclaimed as the 'most reputable and hospitable hotel on the road.' But something was missing. The Cambridge-educated Cornwalls wanted more. What more was summed up in Clement Francis' words: 'However attractive other pursuits and sports may be in their way, hunting must be placed first and the rest nowhere.' They therefore imported foxhounds from England and, lacking the noble fox, went a-hunting the coyote instead. Their sporting pursuits did not keep them from other achievements. Clement Francis became a senator, then the lieutenant-governor of British Columbia, and both brothers regularly presided over local court hearings on such matters as the disputed ownership of a horse or the selling of liquor to the Indians.

DOLL AT COTTONWOOD HOUSE (*right*) The Cariboo of gold-rush times was a rough land, one in which few women ventured to raise families. Traveller Matthew Macfie describes the approach to the roadhouse at Cottonwood in the 1860's: 'The trail worse than it was yesterday. My boots full of water. Dead horses lying in every direction; the wretched animals so overcome with fatigue and deficient feed that they died in the mire. . . . Arrived at Cottonwood at 3 p.m., making only 11 miles journey today.' Yet it was to Cottonwood House that Janet Boyd came in 1868. She married John Boyd, owner of Cottonwood, that year; she was 17. She raised 10 children there, 65 kilometres from the nearest doctor, and was hostess to the many travellers who stayed at the roadhouse. As late as 1930, she still played this role; in that year, the governor-general of Canada and his wife stopped by for a visit. Inevitably known as 'the grand old lady of Cariboo', Janet Boyd died at the age of 89, having outlived her husband and a number of her offspring. The roadhouse over which she presided is now a historic site; with a determined imagination, you can picture the family life of the Boyds in the nineteenth century.

PANDOSY MISSION, KELOWNA—He must have been a familiar sight in the valley, his long black skirts tucked up to reveal corduroy trousers, long grey beard bouncing with each stride of the horse, blanket and bacon behind the saddle, and perhaps the songs of France floating out on the morning air. Father Charles Marie Pandosy first came to the Okanagan Valley in 1859. He and his fellow priest were the first white settlers in the area. The first winter was hard; they ate their horses, baked moss and dried berries and drank a tea made from the leaves of a shrub. They persevered, chose a permanent mission site, built church, house and school, with logs broadaxed from trees they felled. They established the first gardens in a valley that was to become known as the orchard heart of British Columbia. Pandosy planted seeds for apple trees, a variety known as Fallow Waters. The fathers also raised cattle, and grew tobacco, wheat and potatoes. Not forgotten was a vineyard, for Father Pandosy did not scorn the grape. He spent most of the rest of his life at the mission, with the exception of a few years passed at other missions in British Columbia. Throughout those years, he was always on call, riding or walking the Okanagan and Similkameen valleys, tending to the spiritual life of his people. It was one of these trips that caused his death. In 1891, he ventured forth to Keremeos to celebrate a wedding; he caught a chill, and died shortly after his return to Penticton.

O'KEEFE RANCH, VERNON—The buildings of the O'Keefe Ranch in the north Okanagan are the result of a short visit that stretched to 53 years. Cornelius O'Keefe arrived in British Columbia in the 1860's, set to make his fortune in the gold rush. He took a calculated look at the business possibilities, and decided there was more money in servicing the prospectors than in being one. He built and ran the 114 Mile House, a roadhouse on the Cariboo Road. In 1866, he headed south to Oregon, to purchase cattle to drive back to Barkerville and the hungry people there. He took the easy route long since pioneered by the Hudson's Bay brigades, up the Columbia Valley, then by way of the Okanagan. When he reached the north end of the valley, he found fields of tall grass that were perfect for a last fattening of his cattle. A month's stay and he would be headed north once more. But he found the area so pleasant that, instead of leaving, he pre-empted 64 hectares and built a house. In the next 40 years, he expanded his ranch to 1,200 hectares, with grazing land of 6,000, and built the first post office, general store and church in the north Okanagan. Cornelius O'Keefe died in 1919, but the core of the ranch property stayed in the O'Keefe family for another 60 years. Then it was turned over to a charitable foundation, to be opened as an historic site.

OLD FARM MACHINERY, COTTONWOOD HOUSE—Farming in British Columbia was not as surefire as some might have had you believe. On the subject of cattle raising, for example, the CPR public relations department blithely assured the would-be English immigrant, 'the cattle practically look after themselves, and in due course with very little trouble or anxiety, the herd increases and the settler becomes rich.' Nonetheless, the province did present opportunities for the farmer. Like much else that involved a profit, farming beyond the subsistence level began with the Hudson's Bay Company, with company farms supplying agricultural products to residents, Russian traders and the Royal Navy. In the interior, farming began with the gold rush and expanded thereafter, with fruit orchards in the Okanagan, cattle ranches in the Cariboo, dairy farms in the Fraser valley and on Vancouver Island, and waving wheat in Peace River country. Early farm machinery was crude: only hand tools were used until the mid-nineteenth century. Then horse-drawn machines, like this one preserved at Cottonwood House, took over until well into the twentieth century. The provincial Department of Agriculture's report for 1900 shows horse-drawn hay wagons, ploughs and harvesters and cattle roundup by cowboys on horseback. The only exception was a steam-powered thresher. But once the gasoline engine was introduced in about 1915, a new era in farm machinery had begun.

ST. NICHOLAS' CHURCH, SPAHOMIN—They were single-minded men, the missionaries who came to British Columbia to serve their churches and minister to the Indians. 'What joy can be equal to this,' asked one, 'to have a part in the deliverance of whole nations from the power of Satan?' They were as willing to do battle with their own church authorities and other white settlers as they were with the powers of darkness. They saw themselves as protectors of their Indian flocks, stern in their eradication of native practices but determined that other whites would not corrupt the Indians. To this end, some even moved whole communities, establishing model self-sufficient mission towns. St. Nicholas Church is one of the simple wooden churches that these missionaries built throughout British Columbia. A log church covered with cove siding, St. Nicholas lies in the bunchgrass and sage-brush hills near Merritt. With its board-and-batten door and tongued-and-grooved walls, it is a simple construction; like many of its fellows, it was once abandoned, to be replaced by a more modern building. Now, it has been repainted and spruced up, to serve as a gentle reminder of the men who brought their faith to British Columbia and the people who accepted it.

ST. PAUL'S MISSION CHURCH, NORTH VANCOU-
VER (*right*) St. Paul's was the first church built in the
Vancouver area. Chief Snatt of the Squamish Indian band
chose the site. He 'found a few friends (there) camping for
a short time for the purpose of drying and roasting some
of the many ducks that were then easily procured,' and
decided a church should be built at this gathering place.
The first small church was erected in 1866; another, the
basis of the present St. Paul's, replaced it in 1884. The
dedication of this building on a warm and windy June day
in 1886 was overshadowed by another event, the great fire
of Vancouver. As the Indians gathered at the church they
noticed clouds of smoke swept across the water from the
wooden buildings of the new city that had risen on the
other side of the inlet. By the time they could reach their
canoes and cross Burrard Inlet, most of Vancouver had
been destroyed. St. Paul's, when dedicated in 1886, had
only one tower; the second, which made it an official
landmark on charts of Vancouver harbour, was added in
1910. At that time, transepts were also added to the nave
and the church was remodelled in the Gothic style.

WEST COAST RAIN FOREST—The huge trees of the
west coast were a bonanza for early explorers and settlers.
The trees provided replacements for battered ships' spars,
logs for cabins and palisades, and, most important for the
future, raw material for sawmills. The forest giants, with
the Douglas fir as king, grew to a diameter of more than
two metres and a height of more than 60 metres. The first
mills were on Vancouver Island. By the early 1860's there
were mills on the eastern side of Georgia Strait, on both
sides of Burrard Inlet. The best known of the early mill-
owners were two men as different from each other as
could be imagined. The Yankee trader from Maine, Sewell
'Sue' Moody, was industrious, sober, shrewd and ulti-
mately successful. He controlled the town of Moodyville
that grew up around his North Shore mill, allowed no
liquor and stressed the moral life. Englishman Captain
Edward Stamp was argumentative, high-handed and had
little use for 'those damn colonials'. Predictably, the colonials weren't too fond of Stamp, and his mill, near the
future centre of Vancouver, was not successful. In 1869, he
sold out and returned to England; the new mill manager
took one look around the mill town and exclaimed, 'What
is the meaning of this aggregation of filth?' Nonetheless,
the lumber trade in the inlet was booming; in 1864 one
ship had loaded lumber; in 1869 there were 45 that did so.

HASTINGS MILL STORE (*right*) Stamp's Mill was re-named Hastings Mill, and became the centre of settlement in the area that would one day be Vancouver. The Hastings Mill Store, built by Stamp in 1865 to supply the workers and their families, was more than a store. It was the social focus of the neighbourhood, where men and women met to discuss the events of the day, ponder the ways of the world and, almost incidentally, get their shopping done. You could get almost anything at the mill store; groceries, tobacco, pipes, men's suits, overalls, red and blue flannel underwear, patent medicine, hair oil, calico, lace, and linen. In the 1860's, a 45-kilo sack of flour would cost you $1.15, and a fresh rabbit 40 cents. The fire that destroyed every other building in Vancouver some-how missed the mill store. The two-storey clapboard building didn't close for three days and nights straight after the fire, as people tried to replace some of the goods they had lost. Perishables were soon exhausted and men were heard to say they would die happy if they never saw another hardtack biscuit. But they took what they could get in the grey aftermath of the fire. Development in the waterfront area eventually crowded the Hastings Mill Store out of its original site. In 1930 it was barged down the inlet and around the Lions' Gate to its present location, still on the waterfront, at Jericho.

CPR ROUNDHOUSE, VANCOUVER—In the days of steam, roundhouses were as much a fixture of the railways as the tracks themselves. The frequent servicing required by steam engines was provided in these roundhouses, located every 70 kilometres or so along the line. Each roundhouse contained a number of tracks, set in a circle and mounted on a turntable, allowing the engines to enter, be serviced and exit without backing up. The larger roundhouses, like this one in Vancouver, could handle as many as six or eight locomotives at once. Vancouver's roundhouse was built in 1888, and underwent major additions and renovations some 30 years later. It has since become a famous fixture in the False Creek area, though largely unused since diesel took over from steam. Its building was part of the boom that took Vancouver to the front of British Columbia communities. Once it was an-nounced that Vancouver would be the final terminus of the Canadian Pacific Railway tracks, the city, till then little more than a logging town, expanded almost daily, putting paid to the hopes of the other cities—New West-minster, Victoria, Port Moody—that had vied to be the commercial centre of the province.

PORT MOODY RAILWAY STATION—Vancouver won; Port Moody lost. The announcement that Port Moody would be the western terminus of the CPR led to frenzied land speculation and building, as competitors vied for the best locations to profit from the arrival of the steel. The town on Burrard Inlet was proclaimed, as others had been before it, the new commercial centre of the province. Brave words were followed by disappointment. The tracks were extended to the waterfront at Gastown, and Port Moody became just another way station. This wooden station building was not the original stopping place; it replaced the original station in 1905. Just 40 years later the town that welcomed the first passenger train to the west coast welcomed its last. Passenger service to 'PoMo' was suspended in 1945; in 1976 freight service came to an end. The station was closed. A year or two later, it was purchased by the town and moved to a new location, where it became a museum.

RAILWAY TRACKS, THOMPSON RIVER—It's questionable whether John A. Macdonald and his fellow worthy Conservatives knew exactly what they were getting into when they promised British Columbia a transcontinental railway line within 10 years of B.C.'s entry into Confederation. It's doubtful whether they cared. Canada needed British Columbia and Macdonald was convinced of the need for a railway. Building it was a massive undertaking for the young country. East of the Rockies, builders faced muskeg, solid rock and the proverbial miles and miles of miles and miles. The Rockies themselves were a formidable barrier; the eventual route through the Kicking Horse Pass contained grades that seemed suicidal to most railway engineers. Next came the Selkirks, another high and craggy mountain chain. Once out of the mountains, the engineers faced the rivers, fast-flowing and steep-sided. Yet the river valleys and canyons provided the best route to the coast. The transcontinental railway was completed in 1885; 20 years later, the railway builders were at work once more, constructing a second transcontinental railway. The process bankrupted half the companies that set to work on the line and forced a rescue by the federal government and the formation of Canadian National Railways. Both CPR and CNR tracks pass through this section of the Thompson River valley, across the river from each other.

TEMPLE EMANUEL, VICTORIA—The story of British Columbia's early houses of worship is largely Anglican and Catholic. Victoria's temple Emanuel is an exception. Built in the early 1860's when the city's Jewish population was at its peak, it was a multi-faith, multi-city effort. Donations came from city leaders of assorted faiths and from as far away as San Francisco. Greatly prized was a silk wedding canopy, used until recently in Jewish wedding ceremonies at the temple. At the laying of the cornerstone, the Masons marched and the Royal Navy band played; an account of the event took up much of the morrow's front page. Samuel Hoffman, vice-president of the congregation, addressed the crowd who attended:

'Who could not have ridiculed the idea that where, ere now, nought but the hunter's step and the wild beast's roar ever disturbed the wilderness, should at this early day, be erected a synagogue by the scattered tribes of Israel?' In the years following the opening, many of the city's Jewish families left Victoria for the mainland, where Vancouver was taking over as the province's major city. Although a covenant in the land deed provided that the land would be returned to the people of Victoria should there ever be too few for a congregation, Temple Emanuel survived. It was recently restored to its original state, an early example of the use of brick in Victoria.

STATIONMASTER'S HOUSE, PRINCE RUPERT (left) And it came to pass that the moguls of the Grand Trunk sought an outlet on the Pacific Ocean. And they raised the wind and established a city; and the city grew; and the blind pigs waxed fat and were killed off. And the tinhorns prospered.' This newspaper tribute to the genesis of Prince Rupert served the city well enough. Prince Rupert was born of, by and for the railway, in a rush of land speculation and shady dealing that landed the provincial government up to its knees in a muddy scandal. Central to the

scandal was the fact that the said railway moguls had acquired most of the land on Kaien Island in a roundabout deal with the provincial government before they announced that the Grand Trunk terminus would be on the island. Lot prices soared from $50 to $600 in the sudden flowering of a city at the mouth of the Skeena River. The city came fully to life with the completion of the tracks in 1914. Built in 1907, the stationmaster's house was one of the first in town. Home to the stationmaster for most of the years since, it now houses the CNR policeman.

CHINESE PUBLIC SCHOOL, VICTORIA (*left*) Today, this Chinese Public School caters mostly to the children of Chinese-Canadians who fear their cultural heritage will be lost in a homogeneous public school system. These children study after their regular school hours, learning the language, calligraphy, history and geography of China. Ironically, the school was first opened to educate Chinese children who were not welcome in the public school system of 80 years ago. It was built by the Chinese Benevolent Association. The CBA was organized after the completion of the CPR, when anti-Oriental prejudice was strong, jobs for Chinese labourers few and poverty widespread. The association set up a hospital, acquired land for a cemetery, then turned its eyes towards the children. In 1899 it opened a Chinese school, where Chinese students could study full-time. The present school was built in 1907.

THE BUTTER CHURCH, COWICHAN—The old stone church on a hillside above Vancouver Island's Cowichan Bay has no official name. Everyone knows it as the Butter Church, not for its looks but for the method of its financing. Pioneer Oblate missionary Father Peter Rondeault came to Cowichan by canoe from Victoria. For five years he preached where he could, until completion of this church in 1864. The Indians who built the church with the help of a stonemason were paid with the proceeds from butter churned from the milk of Rondeault's two cows. Solidly constructed, with 60-centimetre-thick stone walls, the church was in use for only 10 years. Then a dispute with the Indians on whose land it stood led to its abandonment. It was left to fall into ruins until the walls and roof were restored in 1958. Now its main visitors are tourists and the boys who play lacrosse within the shelter of its sturdy walls.

ST. ANN'S, COWICHAN—Just a few kilometres along the Cowichan Bay Road from the Butter Church stands the church that replaced it. The original St. Ann's burned down late in the nineteenth century. The present classic country church replaced that building. The years and the elements did not treat St. Ann's well. Then, a few years ago, it was restored. Decaying boards were replaced with others cut in the old-fashioned tongued-and-grooved style; the outside of the church was repaired and painted. The inside was painted in muted colours of red and green, to call forth the image of the inner bark of the arbutus tree, Canada's only broad-leafed evergreen, which flourishes in the Cowichan area.

FISGARD LIGHTHOUSE (*right*) It isn't called the wild coast or the lonely coast or the coast of broken dreams. Perhaps it should be. The west coast of Vancouver Island has seen more than its share of ships driven onto the rocks and sailors drowned in the pounding surf. It has seen heroism too, like that of Minnie Patterson, wife of the lighthouse keeper at Cape Beale, who ran eight kilometres through water and over the rough trail to Bamfield to summon help for the foundering barque *Coloma*. The coast's potential for trouble was recognized early. Dispatches in the early 1850's from colonial governor James Douglas called repeatedly for the building of lighthouses.

The Fisgard light, at the entrance to Esquimalt Harbour on the southern tip of the island, was the first to turn on its beacon. This light allowed ships to enter harbour at night, and helped sailors in stormy weather. It was one of a chain of lighthouses built along the island coast. Eventually a lifesaving trail, with cabins and telegraph, was cleared along the coast. Initially, Fisgard was manned by a keeper, but was converted to automatic operation in 1929. It still marks the harbour entrance, 'showing bright when bearing from N. to W. to N. 60 to W. and red from W. 60W to S.6E.'

IVANHOE TUGBOAT—For 54 years, the *Ivanhoe* plied the Georgia Strait and Inside Passage, usually with a sizeable raft of logs attached. Tow boats have always been a part of the coastal logging industry. Even with the move to dry-land storage, log booms are still an identifying feature of the west coast. The *Ivanhoe* was one of the last boats built at Vancouver's False Creek. In more than half a century of work, she probably towed more logs than any other boat on the coast. She was a steam tug until her conversion to diesel in 1937. In a nice merging of interests, original owner Ronald Wilson used coal from a mine he owned at Merritt to fire the tug's steam engines. For most of her life, the *Ivanhoe* worked for a McMillan Bloedel company. She was kept on the water by the general manager of Kingcome Navigation and by her crew; when the manager retired, so did the *Ivanhoe*. Not forever, though. She is now being restored and will go on display, possibly in the False Creek area where she was launched down the slipway.

LEGISLATIVE BUILDINGS, VICTORIA—Even in its architects, British Columbia had to be a little flamboyant. Francis Mawson Rattenbury arrived in B.C. in the 1890's, determined to become rich and famous. In his own way, he did both. Announcing that he had worked for a preeminent British architect who had actually died before Rattenbury was of age, the brash 25-year-old swept all competition before him and was awarded the contract for the new Legislative Buildings. In the next 20 years, he designed the Empress Hotel; the Vancouver, Nanaimo and Nelson courthouses; and any number of other public buildings, most of them imposing stone edifices. He speculated in land sales, founded a transportation company he thought could dominate traffic to the Klondike, tried to ship salmon to the South Pacific, and dabbled in a number of other get-rich-quick schemes. He and his wife missed the official opening of the Legislative Buildings, because they were on a jaunt over the Chilkoot Pass to Klondike, just to show how simple the trip could be. But Rattenbury's death brought him far greater fame than his life. He was bludgeoned to death by his second wife's chauffeur-lover; the resulting trial shocked England and is considered one of the classics of the century. Not everyone was perturbed by the murder. 'The deceased conceived and built that amazing pile of architectural inconsequence at Victoria,' wrote a Vancouver newspaper columnist, referring to the Legislative Buildings. 'That in itself should be sufficient excuse for the lady.... The conclusion of this drama should be a warning to all architects.'

48

CRAIGDARROCH CASTLE, VICTORIA—It might be true that Robert Dunsmuir promised to build his wife a castle if she would come with him from Scotland to British Columbia. It's more likely that the reason for Craigdarroch was less romantic; the millionaire coal baron of Vancouver Island, whose name was linked with strike-breaking, lockouts, mines and mine explosions, wanted a home that would rival those on San Francisco's Snob Hill. He didn't survive to live in his castle, dying of pneumonia just before it was finished. His widow moved in however in 1890 and gained a reputation as a reclusive matriarch. Joan Olive White Dunsmuir's name appears in few newspapers of the day; it is absent even in the account of the sumptuous wedding of her daughter to Sir Robert Mus-

grave. She changed her retiring habits when her son Alexander died, and left his possessions to his brother, James. She and Alexander's widow contested the will in a bitterly-fought five-year court battle. From then on, mother and son did not speak, although at one point they lived across the road from each other. When Joan died in 1908, no one wanted her castle. The 33-room edifice was a white elephant. Two years later, it was raffled off, a chance going to each buyer of a lot on the subdivided grounds around Craigdarroch. It became, in turn, a services hospital, college classrooms and school board offices. In the 1970's, it was restored to its role as Victoria's only castle, and was opened to the public.

NELSON COURTHOUSE (*left*) With the raunchy reputations of the mining camps in their thoughts, the good people of the Kootenays yearned for a little respectability. None wanted it more than the residents of Nelson, self-styled the Queen City. Stability and solidity were what was needed, to counteract the transient nature of boom towns and dust dreams. The merchants and society leaders of Nelson built with brick and stone, with the result that this city now has more designated heritage buildings

than anywhere in the province outside Vancouver and Victoria. For their courthouse, constructed at the insistence of the local Conservative Club, they brought in architect Rattenbury. Designed in Richardsonian Romanesque style, the solid stone replaced a wooden building and brought to the administration of justice a proper weight and dignity. When the courthouse was completed in 1909, Nelson's place as administrative centre for the West Kootenay was assured.

SANDON—Lies and mistrust marked the birth of Sandon; fire, water and the end of silver brought its death. The story started in the 1890's, when two prospectors were slogging home through the bush to Kaslo after an unsuccessful prospecting trip. They came across what looked like a promising silver vein near Carpenter Creek and chipped out samples to take back for assay. Great was one partner's disappointment when the other showed him the assay reports; the samples tested so poorly there was no point in returning to the site. In low spirits, the prospector headed for the bar. There, he heard that his former partner had just left town in a great hurry, heading for points unknown with a new partner. Figuring out the doublecross he found four new partners himself and the five of them harnessed up and headed out. The five won the race and staked the richest claims around what would be Sandon. Sandon became the heart of the Silver Slocan—bars and eating houses open 24 hours a day, seven days a week; people sleeping in shifts at the hotels;

brokers' offices, stores, banks, even an opera house. One feature made it unique among mining towns—its main street was built on a boardwalk over Carpenter Creek. Fire struck Sandon the first blow, destroying most of its buildings in 1900. There was enough optimism remaining to rebuild the town, but Sandon was virtually abandoned a few years later when the silver vein petered out. For a few brief years in the 1940's, Sandon was home to those relocated from the coast in Canada's ugly move against Japanese-Canadians during the Second World War. After the war, they, too, left, and when the Carpenter broke loose in 1955, collapsing most of the remaining buildings, few were left to mourn. Recluses and dreamers still come to live at Sandon, to hide like hermits or to cater to the occasional tourist intent on exploring a ghost town. But they are not enough to breath life into the remains of the town. There will be no reincarnation of Sandon's boisterous past.

HATLEY PARK (*left*) If there was ever a British Columbia family dynasty fit for melodrama, it was the Dunsmuirs. Father a strong-willed captain of industry, his widow almost a hermit, one prodigal son, one son who ruled the province, mansions, castles, a battle over a will, rumours and money; the Dunsmuirs had them all. Premier, then governor-general, son James had as great a name in government as his father had in industry. His monument is Hatley Park, just outside Victoria. Designed by architect Samuel McClure, the park and the mansion were the finest on Vancouver Island. The grounds contained ornamental lakes stocked with trout, Japanese and Italian gardens, a home farm, stables with 14 hunters imported from En-

gland, and staff of four white gardeners and 100 Chinese. The house was no letdown. Within were an oak-panelled dining room, a library, a Persian room, a billiard room, a gunroom, a ballroom, a tower room with a picture of Mephistopheles. Whatever you wished to do, you could find a room dedicated to that purpose at Hatley Park. To serve the family there were, among others, a Chinese cook and an English butler. When James Dunsmuir died, no one wanted to keep Hatley Park in the style to which it had become accustomed. The estate was sold to the federal government for use as a military college. The gardens are open to the public, for those who want to see a little of the magnificence engendered by the Dunsmuir dynasty.

52 KASLO VILLAGE HALL (*right*) The tombstone on the front page of the Kaslo newspaper was black-bordered: 'Busted by Gosh. Keep off the grass. Sacred to the memory of the Kaslo claim. Born May 12, 1893, died August 25, 1893. Aged sixteen weeks. Let her R.I.P.' It was a whimsical tribute to the death of a dream by a newspaper editor who published unpaid ads upside down and half-paid ones sideways. The death of the claim didn't mean the death of Kaslo, that was always more of a supply town than a mining centre itself. Kaslo was founded in the 1890's, with the Slocan silver rush. The steamers chugged up the lake to its dock, to transfer passengers and cargo to the narrow-gauge Kaslo and Slocan railway line. This village hall, wood-framed on a stone foundation, was built in 1898. Kaslo flourished while the rush was on, then slipped back into a quiet lakeside existence when the mining camps became ghost towns. Recently, most of its turn-of-the-century buildings have been restored, making the town a period piece by the side of Kootenay Lake.

S.S. *MOYIE*—She was the last of the Kootenay steamers, broadbeamed and chunky, running the lake with paddlewheel churning and whistle a-toot. The S.S. *Moyie* was launched in Nelson in 1898; for 59 years, she served Nelson, Kaslo, Lardeau, Argenta, and waypoints, criss-crossing the long narrow lake to pick up and deliver passengers, freight and mail. She was one of the many sternwheelers of British Columbia's early days, boats that appeared wherever there was a boom town or a burgeoning settlement near navigable water. They served the gold rush, the Slocan silver rush, the Skeena, the Arrow Lakes. These lakes of the Kootenay seemed to be their natural habitat. Long and narrow, wedged between mountain ranges, they provided a natural transportation route. The steamers transported miners and goods for the mining towns, but they outlasted most of the towns. They carried passengers and freight and mail and horse teams and grand pianos wherever there was no road or rail. The *Moyie* ran on the CPR's Inland Lake and River service longer than all the rest, until 1957. By then, the elegant dining room and the 14 passenger cabins had been put to other uses. When she retired, there were enough people who remembered the best days of the sternwheelers to insist that she not be sold for scrap. She's a museum now, beached at Kaslo, beside the lake she once as good as owned.

ROSSLAND MINERS' HALL (*left*) Force was met with force in the mining towns of the western United States in the 1890's. If mine owners hired scabs to crack heads and take miners' jobs, then miners retaliated with clubs and stones. Among the most radical and militant of the miners' unions was the Western Federation of Miners. This union moved into British Columbia in 1895; its first local in Rossland was just as militant but a good deal less violent than in the United States. Here, the government seemed to be somewhat on the miners' side; it enacted legislation enforcing an eight-hour day. The mine owners agreed, but announced they would pay an hourly rate, reducing pay from that received for the 10-hour day. Within months, there were 10 new union locals in the Kootenays; shortly thereafter, the miners walked out on strike. They won that battle, but the mine owners continued the war. In 1901, the union locals were out again, in a strike aimed at putting an end to company attempts to crush the unions. This time, the miners lost the battle but won the war. The strike collapsed and the company successfully sued the union for damages—among the spoils was this Rossland union hall—but the strike did result in amendments to the Trade Unions Act that were favourable to the workers.

GREENWOOD SLAG—The slag piles and hollow slag bells that lie just outside Greenwood hearken back to the days when British Columbia interests first took on the world in the smelting of copper. The British Columbia Copper Company opened the first smelter in 1901, in the Kootenays, and within a month claimed a world record for the amount of copper smelted in 24 hours. Its entry onto the market spurred the established companies to dump copper, hoping to drive down prices and put the upstart out of business. The fall in prices hurt B.C. Copper, but did not kill it. The Greenwood smelter survived until the nearby mines ran out of copper in 1919. Operations at those mines were straightforward, but a nearby claim spawned one of the 'brave-new-world' schemes with which early British Columbia abounded. Volcanic Brown staked his claim on a mountainside and announced he would build Volcanic City for those who would work his mine. The city would be closed to the three curses of mankind—banks, churches and schools. Regrettably for the experiment, the vein at the intended site was worthless and Volcanic Brown moved on. He disappeared on a prospecting trip some years later, while searching for the legendary lost mine of Slumach. His body was never found. Wherever it rests, you may be sure there are no bankers, priests, or teachers.

MOYIE CHURCH & GRAVESTONE, MOYIE CHURCHYARD—The Kootenay village of Moyie has one of the very few churches in British Columbia build as part of the payment for a mining claim. At the turn of the century, Father Nicholas Coccola, an Oblate missionary in charge of the St. Eugene Mission, told the Indians who came to the mission that he would like to be informed if they came across any deposits of the lead and silver ore, galena. Not long after, an Indian named Pierre brought in some rocks to show the priest. Coccola, Pierre and mining entrepreneur James Cronin laid claim to the appropriate area, and Cronin developed the claim over the next three years. The mine, known as the St. Eugene, was then sold to an American company for $22,000. Thirty years later, Coccola described the results of the sale. 'A model house was built for Pierre, who also received cattle, farm implements, and $5 a month from Cominco. A beautiful Gothic church was erected at the mission and another in Moyie.'

57

MOYIE FIREHALL—Fire was always the enemy. The mining camps were thrown up so rapidly, so flimsily, and with the buildings so close together, they fell easily prey to flames that might flare from wood touching an overheated stovepipe, a match carelessly dropped or, as legend had it in the Barkerville fire, an iron knocked over when a miner tried to steal a kiss from a dancehall girl. The people of Moyie wanted to guard against a like fate for their town. They formed a volunteer fire brigade and built a firehall to house the hand trucks that were the forerunners of today's fire engine. This larger hall was built in 1907, and was graced with a clanging bell that would summon the fire-fighters should flames be spotted. Moyie was spared destruction by fire. It could not be spared the other common fate of mining towns. When the silver ran out, so did the miners, and Moyie became another one of the Kootenays' near-ghost-towns.

GABRIOLA (*right*) Benjamin Tingley Rogers was a West Coast baron with a sweet touch. Not content at the age of 22 with managing a sugar refinery for someone else, he left the United States for eastern Canada, where he persuaded backers to invest in a refinery in Vancouver. By the time he was 24, the British Columbia Sugar Refinery was producing sugar for shipment by rail and sea. Over the next 10 years, Rogers married the niece of one of his backers, acquired the title of 'The Sugar King' and constructed what was declared to be the finest private home in the province. Rogers hired Samuel McClure, the best-known West Coast residential architect, who was restrained whereas Rattenbury was flamboyant, and was determined to create a natural British Columbia style whereas Rattenbury wanted to transplant European grandeur. The home that McClure designed for Rogers was Gabriola, a handsome stone residence in Vancouver's west end. Built with stone quarried from Gabriola Island, near Nanaimo, the mansion featured B.C.'s first full concrete basement, 17 fireplaces, a conservatory, a gazebo and a *porte-cochère*—where, presumably, Rogers halted his electric car after trips such as the one along a bicycle path that saw him sentenced to a fine of $5 or 10 days in jail. The report doesn't say which punishment Rogers chose. Gabriola also contained stained glass windows designed and created by Vancouver's Bloomfield brothers. Charles, the artisan, and James, the artist, rarely worked together, but the Gabriola windows, one of their few joint projects, are a happy result of the combination of their talents.

MANHATTAN APARTMENTS, VANCOUVER DOWNTOWN—The Manhattan was the first appearance of a phenomenon that eventually took over downtown and west end Vancouver: the apartment building. Built in 1908, the four-storey building was intended by owner William Lamont Tait to be the best apartment block in the city. The interior corridors were decorated with a frieze in embossed metal; the block displayed stained glass windows, an ornate pilastered entrance and an electric elevator. The ground floor was reserved for shops. High atop the building was a restaurant-teahouse. The 360-degree view from the teahouse was not blocked by central kitchens; all food was prepared in the basement and sent to the diners via dumb waiter. In later years, the Manhattan fell on difficult times, and the owners sought to tear it down and rebuild on what had become prime real estate. Tenants wouldn't have it; some camped for months without heat or hot water in the crumbling building. They won. The building was restored, partly by the owners and partly by a tenants' co-operative. It subsequently won a cross-Canada award for the best preservation of an old building maintaining commercial and living space, to show that 'old buildings don't have to be museums.'

FORT STEELE—The North West Mounted Police made only one foray into British Columbia. In 1887, with no police in the area, there were reports of trouble between whites and Indians in the east Kootenay. Orders came for Sam Steele and his men to leave their prairie base and cross the mountains, their destination the Kootenay River. The troubles had begun when two Indians were thrown into jail, accused of the murder of two white placer miners. Convinced that his men were innocent but that their chances with white man's justice were slim, Kootenay chief Isadore and his followers released the men. A mild uproar ensued; it was Steele of the Mounted to the rescue. The colonel arrived and ordered Isadore to produce the accused men. Isadore complied. 'I was pleased with the bearing of the Indians, both accused and witnesses,' Steele wrote in his memoirs. 'They showed great intelligence and it was clear that they knew nothing of the murder which was probably committed by some loose character frequenting the trails.' The men were released. Steele and his troop proceeded to build a fort at the confluence of the Kootenay River and Wild Horse Creek, a fort that was named for Steele. The stay of the mounted police was short. By the following year, they had returned to the prairies. Fort Steele remained. It became a focus for commerce when the North Star silver vein was discovered and mined not far away. Steamboats ran the Kootenay to Fort Steele: 'Give a Kootenay pilot a heavy

dew and his boat will arrive on schedule,' they said of the sternwheelers. The dew must have been too light. Two steamboats were wrecked on the river; that and the building of railway tracks to nearby Cranbrook ended Fort Steele's run. North Star ore was shipped to a smelter at Trail instead of down the river, and the government offices were moved from Fort Steele to Cranbrook. The fort was officially dead. It came to life again only 60 years later, when the government declared it a historic site and began restoring the remaining buildings and moving others of an appropriate era to the fort, to create a replica of a turn-of-the-century Kootenay town.

62

COCKTAIL SHAKER, PRINCETON MUSEUM—
Drink, evil drink, a curse and much worse—but you
would never have persuaded the early miners of that. If
there was one miner, he had a flask; if there were two, one
would start a saloon. The short-lived boom town of
Granite Creek, near Princeton, was no exception. It was
founded on booze; local cowboys drinking in a bar below
the United States border started the rumour that there was
gold to be found in them thar hills. Then they reeled back
home, laughing their heads off to see the stampede they
had started. The rumour-starting wasn't unusual, and
neither was the reaction. There's a story of two miners in
Heaven who tell their fellow angels where gold can be
found on earth. Within minutes, they have the clouds to
themselves, as all the would-be prospectors descend on
the site. After a while, one of the instigators starts to pack
his gear. 'Where are you going?' asks the other. 'We
started that story.' 'I know,' says the first. 'But it just
might be true.' In Granite Creek, the rumour did turn out
to be true. One of the Americans found gold at the creek.
The instant town that sprang up attracted the raunchiest,
rowdiest group of cowboys turned prospectors it was ever
a town's bad luck to find. By late 1885, there were 'two
licensed houses for the sale of liquor', by the next spring
there were 10. But by October, 'six whiskey shops (had)
closed up since spring.' Whether there was more gold
mined or whiskey drunk is an interesting question—as is
that of what a cocktail shaker was doing in a town that
didn't set much store by the social niceties.

CALENDAR PAGE FROM PRINCETON BILLIARD
ROOM (*right*) The number of 'respectable ladies' in a
backwoods town was small indeed. Even if you added in
the women who were in town to do a different sort of
prospecting, men vastly outnumbered women. Perhaps
that was the reason why these misty, romantic portraits
were so popular in saloon, hotel and billiard parlour.
Many a miner with aching head and empty pocket, the
results of indulging too well but not too wisely, may have
looked with longing at pinups such as these.

QUILCHENA HOTEL—The newly opened Quilchena Hotel was a fine hostelry, with porches, dormer windows, mahogany beds, bridal suite, a billiard saloon, a polo ground, and food that was 'the best in the West'. It lacked only guests. The three-storey hotel was built in 1907 by a rancher who owned large sections of the surrounding land. He was convinced that guests would come by coach and carriage to visit his opulent inn. He was also convinced that a branch line of the railway would soon be built from Kamloops to Princeton, and that the line would pass close by the Quilchena. He was wrong on both accounts. There were few overnight guests, and the hotel had to subsist on proceeds from its bar—a bar with no chairs, on the basis that if a man couldn't stay standing up, he'd had enough. The year 1919 brought prohibition and the Quilchena closed. It remained closed until 1958; when it reopened, the polo ground was converted to a golf course, nearby hunting and fishing were the major attractions, and automobile passengers were the main customers. The bar and room furnishings, however, remained much as they had been 50 years before.

IRRIGATION FLUMES, WALLACHIN (*left*) By the twentieth century, the day of the English city-dweller turned immigrant farmer seemed to have passed. But some images persist beyond their time and the image of riches to be gained in the fertile reaches of Canada appealed to the group of English settlers who tried to convert the dry benchlands above the Thompson River near Kamloops into green farms. The Thompson had water aplenty, but the task of raising it to their farm fields was beyond the settlers. Instead, they dammed Deadman Creek to the north, and build more than a dozen kilometres of wooden flumes and trestles to carry water to their apple orchards and potato fields. The colony was probably doomed from the beginning, for the land was not of much use for intensive farming, and the flumes were badly designed. The First World War sealed Wallachin's fate. Many of the men went away to fight, and the flumes were damaged by storms. The colony crumpled. The remaining settlers moved away. All that is left now of their dream is a few stunted apple trees and the scattered remnants of the flumes.

KILBY GENERAL STORE—'The last of the old-time general stores,' Acton Kilby used to tell his visitors as he showed them around the pack-rat rooms in the white building north of the Fraser River. Son of the man who started the store in 1904, Kilby kept it running, half museum, half merchandise, until his death in 1978. Its location, Harrison Mills, was a train stop in the early years of the century, a place where steam engines took on coal and water. Passengers would descend from the carriages, cross the gangway over the tracks and take refreshment at the counter of Thomas Kilby's temperance hotel and general store. And what could they find on the counters and shelves of the store? Penny candies, coal-oil soap, bins of flour, sugar and other staples, elixirs and remedies, cough syrup whose primary ingredient was alcohol, dry goods and sewing needles, an assortment that today's department store would be glad to boast.

THREE VALLEY GAP GENERAL STORE—Many mourn the death of the general store, pointing out that those remaining are usually operated as museums or, like this one at Three Valley Gap near Revelstoke, part of historic re-creations. It's true that the genial storekeeper with the wire-rim glasses may never again pore over his accounts by the light of a coal-oil lamp, dispense advice on snake-oil remedies or dispense supplies from bulk barrels beside the pot-bellied stove. But there still remains many an echo of the general store in British Columbia. You won't travel far in the province without coming upon one of the store cum post office cum gas station combinations that are the social and commercial centres of many small communities. On Gulf Island, in logging camp or at isolated ranch-country crossroads, the general store is far from dead.

Apple branches on wall of Doukhobor brick house

DOUKHOBOR VILLAGE—Everyone had a reason for coming to British Columbia. The Doukhobors' was simpler than most—they wanted to be left alone. This religious sect was a community unto itself, wishing to live by its own rules without interference from the state. They would not fight for the country in which they lived, would not send their children to state schools, and did not want to pay taxes. They found little tolerance in their native land of Russia, where they were persecuted for their refusal to serve in the armies of the Czar. They sought homes in other countries, asking for promises that they would not have to act in ways contrary to their beliefs. Some came to western Canada, with the understanding that the Canadian government had given them freedom to follow the dictates of their consciences. By 1912, some 5,000 had moved to the valleys of the West Kootenay in British Columbia. Here they established communal villages, each one home for 35 to 40 people and each centred on 40 hectares of land. They built roads, bridges, saw mills, irrigation systems and reservoirs. They planted orchards of thousands of trees. They prospered in peace until the 1930's, living a life symbolized in the words with which they closed each meeting: 'Calm and peaceful, calm and peaceful, we will all go home' and by the phrase, 'toil and a peaceful life'. Two things shattered that peace. The first was the Depression. The second was the rise of the Doukhobor sect called the Sons of Freedom, whose leaders and consciences told them they must burn their own buildings and those of others and protest against the materialism of life by shedding their clothes. It's a sad irony that a group that believed so strongly in peace should have been made famous by dissenters who turned to violence. There are still many Doukhobors living in the West Kootenay, but little remains of the communal lifestyle. Some of the characteristic two-storey red brick houses that were once the centres of their villages can still be found in the valleys between Grand Forks and Castlegar.

GASSY JACK STATUE AND BYRNES BLOCK, GASTOWN—When Gassy Jack paddled his canoe round Brockton Point and headed for the clearing in the tall trees, his mind was more on prosperity than posterity. He was leaving, not to say fleeing from, an embarrassing mix-up with a former partner in a New Westminster watering place. He had decided to start a saloon near Hastings Mill, some five kilometres by water plus 15 by road from the nearest drinking establishment. Gassy Jack Deighton, so-named for his garrulity, is considered by many to be the founder of Vancouver; he was certainly the founder of the settlement of Gastown, beside Burrard Inlet. He set up his barroom less than a kilometre from mill property, and was rewarded by the nightly arrival of mill workers, ready to relax. He had a good thing while it lasted. 'I was here one year and a half before anyone found out I was making money finally it was found out, and then a rush,' he wrote to his brother. 'Hotels, Saloons, Stores and everyone going to make a pile and run me out but they did not succeed.' Gassy Jack's success was his downfall; competitors arrived, then law and order. He opened a hotel with his saloon, then went back for a time to working as a Fraser River pilot. When Gastown was surveyed, his saloon lay in the middle of an intersection. He built his second hotel not far away. He died in 1875, and was arrayed in finery for his funeral—a new white shirt, underdrawers and necktie. After the fire of 1886 that destroyed Vancouver, the Byrnes Block was erected on the site of Deighton's second hotel; its first use was as the Alhambra Hotel, the first in town to offer rooms at more than one dollar a night.

SAM KEE BUILDING, VANCOUVER CHINATOWN—
Gassy Jack was a character about whom myths grew; Sam
Kee was a mythical character. His name is borne by
Vancouver's narrowest building but Sam Kee never existed. The name was simply a convenient *nom de plume*
for Shun Moon and Tang Toy, principals in the Sam Kee
trading company. One of the wealthiest merchant firms in
Vancouver in the early 1900's, the company was involved
in real estate, manufactured charcoal, contracted Chinese
labour, operated a herring saltery and ran an export-
import business. The company owned a strip of land on
Pender Street, in Vancouver's Chinatown. When the city
widened the street, they cut the land available for building
to less than one and a half metres wide. The company was
undeterred; a shop building the width of the property and
30 metres long was constructed back-to-back with an
existing tenement. Bay windows on the second storey
overhung the ground by almost a metre, and a basement
containing steam baths extended below the sidewalk.
Shown here reflected in the windows of the Sam Kee
Building is the *Chinese Times* building across the street,
another Chinatown pioneer. The oldest Chinese newspaper still in existence in Canada, the *Times* is handset by
typesetters who carefully lift out individual characters
from the ranks serried before them.

ROWLATT FARMSTEAD, SURREY—These farm buildings, constructed in the 1890's, belonged for more than 60 years to a man with a rare skill. Leonard Rowlatt was a water-diviner who located sites for more than 1,000 wells in the Fraser Valley near his home. English-born Rowlatt came to British Columbia in 1907, buying the farmstead that bears his name a few years later. He gloried in the past; his farm was home to every artifact he could discover, including a surrey with a fringe on top that he drove in local parades until his death at the age of 85. Rowlatt was well known for his collection, but better known for his water divining. Scorning the forked stick of water-dowsing tradition, he used his hands held out in front of him to guide him to hidden water sources. 'When I hit a stream, it feels like my whole stomach jumped up,' he used to tell inquirers. He seemed to know at just what depth the water lay, and delighted in confounding those who said that water-divining could not work. His greatest triumph came when all conventional methods of finding water on a new hospital site had failed. Rowlatt came, divined, pointed. The machines dug. Water welled up. No one was surprised—least of all Leonard Rowlatt himself.

HANEY HOUSE—A Cape Breton lad who learned the brickmaking trade in Ontario and came to British Columbia by way of California was responsible for this house overlooking the Fraser River. Thomas Haney explored both sides of the river in the 1870's, looking for clay that was suitable for brickmaking. In 1877, he bought 400 hectares of land for $1,000 and over the next few years started a farm, a brickworks and a livery stable. Several other brickworks were built in the same area. Chinese labourers dug the clay, wheeled it on carts to the plant, took away the finished bricks, and loaded them on scows for transportation downriver. Haney became enough of a local celebrity that a school holiday was declared on his death and the town near his original farm bears his name.

LONDON FARMHOUSE, RICHMOND—Though most of British Columbia's terrain was less than ideal for agriculture, some areas were close to perfect. The islands of the Fraser delta were among these. Formed by silt carried downstream by the river and dumped at the river mouth, the islands were flat, their soil was rich, and access to them was easy. By the late 1870's, a number of farmers had begun cultivating the area. In 1881 the London brothers arrived, buying 80 hectares on Lulu Island for $25 a hectare. Charles and William London built this house, started a store, operated a post office called Londons Landing, and built a wharf from which they could ship out farm crops and receive supplies. That they chose their land wisely was borne out in a comment from the editors of the following year's B.C. Directory. Speaking of Richmond, they commented, 'Even with comparatively careless cultivation, enormous yields are realized, and an accurate statement of what the land will do in this respect, would sound like romance.' The islands did require dyking, since most of the land was within two metres of sea level. Those parts which have not been taken over by suburban housing still bear out the optimism of the original settlers, as the Richmond fields produce heavy crops of small fruits such as cranberries, blueberries and strawberries, and of a wide variety of vegetables.

BURR HOUSE, DEAS ISLAND (*left*) Burr House is part of B.C.'s Irish heritage. Two families of Burrs arrived here from Ireland in 1859. The head of one became the keeper of an insane asylum, while the other took up farming. In 1905, a son of the farmer built Burr House, a Queen-Anne-style dwelling with a gabled porch, turned verandah posts and a dining table with 11 separate leaves that could seat 28. In the 1980's, Burr House became front-page copy. It was threatened with destruction, wrangled over and, at length, rescued and declared a historic site. One of the conditions of the rescue was that the house be moved to Deas Island, less than a kilometre away and still on the banks of the Fraser River. Hydraulic jacks were used to lever the house onto the moving truck—but the truck wasn't moving for long. A low telephone cable blocked progress, and house and truck spent the night by the side of the road. The cable was removed the next day, and the house reached its final destination in a heritage park on the island.

76 NORTH PACIFIC CANNERY, PORT EDWARD—'The room in which the cooking was performed was, in temperature, like a Turkish bath; no windows or doors were allowed to be opened, except of necessity, under the mistaken impression that the cold currents of air would injure the product.' Thus Frederick Howay, pioneer British Columbia historian, described one of the first attempts at salmon canning in the province. Salted and barrelled salmon had been exported since the Hudson's Bay Company's early days at Fort Langley, but canning did not begin on a large scale until late in the century. At the industry's peak, there were 18 canneries operating at the Skeena mouth—including North Pacific—and 49 on the channels of the Fraser delta. North Pacific was built in 1889 by the North Pacific Canning Company, then sold in 1891 to Anglo-British Columbia Packing Company. Anglo-British Columbia, under the ownership of Henry Bell-Irving, acquired nine canneries between 1890 and 1894; and by 1894, it was boasting a profit of £22,000 and was canning almost one-quarter of the total salmon packed in B.C. The North Pacific complex of warehouses, sheds, machine shops and houses was built in large part on a platform over the water, supported by wooden pilings driven into the wood below. It closed in 1968; there are still some hopes that it may reopen one day as a museum for the fishing and canning industries.

MENDING NETS, PORT EDWARD—From Fraser to Skeena and beyond, at every fishing village in between, the pale turquoise nets are looped on bars and stanchions, ready for inspection. For what was true at the start of the commercial fishery a hundred years ago remains true today: the catch can be no better than the quality of the net. Frayed line must be repaired, gaps closed, foreign matter removed. Though the routine hasn't changed, the nets have. Nylon has replaced cotton twine, gill nets have grown in length, and the purse-seine that was drawn tight from a tiny scow set loose from the mother ship has given way to a giant drum-seine set by the big ships of the fleet. Yet despite the mechanization of much of the fishing industry, the essential task of net-mending remains a job for skilful human hands.

CRAB TRAPS, STEVESTON—'Whelks, cockles, clams and crabs are to be had in large quantities,' was the word from an 1891 Natural History Society of British Columbia report. Were these crustaceans valued? Not at all. '(They) are largely used by the Indians, who prefer the clam as bait when trolling for salmon.' So much for the spiny-clawed crab. But, like many a once-despised product of the sea, the crab has come into its own. Now each year between 1,000 and 2,000 tonnes of crab are caught; most of them are exported, either live, canned or frozen. The crabs are caught in these circular stainless-steel-mesh traps. The traps are baited with clams or fish flesh, then placed on the sea bottom, each marked with a coloured plastic float attached to a line.

FISH BOAT, HOWE SOUND—A jungle of masts at the fishermen's wharf, lonely spars on a rolling sea, white hulls massed at the start of another season—fish boats have been a feature of the British Columbia coast since the beginning of the commercial fishery. The first boats were small, powered by oars or sails. In the boom years of the fisheries at the turn of the century, cannery tugboats would tow a long line of these boats upriver toward the sea. The tug shrilled out its signal and the boat captains hastened to hook on to the towline. Some men and women were still making a living by 'rowboating' as late as the 1930's; aboard these five-metre double-enders, with a sprit sail for travelling from place to place, they trolled the inshore grounds with line, lead and home-made spinner blades. Now, as then, boats are still classified as trollers, gill-netters and seiners, but how they have grown! Now they carry the most sophisticated electronic equipment and the highest price tags. Including licenses, even a second-hand gillnetter will cost upwards of $70,000, an average seiner can cost close to half a million and the pride of the fleet, a freezer trawler to catch, process and freeze fish on board, cost $3.4 million in the late 1970's.

ROOFS OF HYCROFT—It was built in the first decade of the century and, for more than 20 years, invitations to social events held at Hycroft were the most sought-after in Vancouver. The New Year's Eve masquerade balls were famous, and anyone worth knowing in city society was bound to be there. Hycroft, built for General Alexander Duncan McCrae, had 12 fireplaces, most of them in Italian marble but one in sandstone with the McCrae family crest carved on it. There were four solariums, and a fireproof, burglar-proof, wine cellar protected by three separate double-locked doors. The Prince of Wales once played handball in the recreation building which contained, as

well as the handball court, a swimming pool, bowling alley and squash court. By the 1940's, it no longer seemed possible to live in the Hycroft style and General, now Senator, McCrae gave the building to the federal government for use as a veterans' hospital. 'There will be fewer structures of this kind in Canada in future,' said McCrae on that occasion. 'With more equal distribution of wealth and taxes, those more fortunate will have to share with others.' The account does not record whether he was abashed or impressed by this trend. Since 1962, Hycroft has been the home of the University Women's Club.

GLENBRAE (*right*) It was to be a reminder of the Scotland left behind—Glenbrae, the valley by the mountains. For lumber and real-estate magnate William Lamont Tait, the twin-towered mansion in the fashionable neighbourhood of Shaughnessy was but a brief stopping place. He died in 1919, just nine years after the house was completed. Glenbrae featured wrought iron railings overlaid with gold leaf rosettes, brought from Scotland; a padding of

seaweed underlaid the ballroom floor. The years after Tait died were not favourable to the Glenbrae lifestyle. The house was sold or rented out to a variety of owners and tenants. For a brief period of 11 months in the 1920's, it was home to the Kanadian Knights of the Ku Klux Klan, a group whose activities must have startled the sedate and moneyed folk of Shaughnessy. Now Glenbrae is a private hospital for the elderly.

ROEDDE HOUSE, VANCOUVER—Gustav Adolph Roedde was Vancouver's first bookbinder. An immigrant from Germany, he first worked for the Queen's Printer in Victoria, then moved to Vancouver to open his own firm. His house, which some claim was one of the few private residences designed by Francis Mawson Rattenbury, was built in Vancouver's West End in 1894. The distinctive turret on top was planned to give Matilda Roedde the same kind of view she once had enjoyed at her North Sea island home.

FAIRVIEW HOUSE (*left*) Built in 1890, Fairview House was one of the first residences on the hill overlooking Vancouver's downtown. Sir John Watt Reid, a military doctor who served in the Crimean and China wars and the Ashanti campaign, and Lady Georgina Reid, first president of the Vancouver Council of Women, were the house's first owners. The Reids remained in British Columbia for only six years after the doctor's retirement in 1899. They then returned to England, where Reid was appointed honorary physician to Edward VII. At its inception one of the ritzier suburbs of Vancouver, Fairview declined over the years until it consisted mostly of crumbling rooming houses and the remains of once-proud mansions. Then, in the 1970's, its spectacular views of downtown and the North Shore mountains, and urban renewal in False Creek below, brought renewed interest. Many of the older houses were restored as offices and residences, and it once more became one of the sought-after locations in the city.

DRAUGHT HORSES, FRASER VALLEY—Pulling the stagecoach, carrying supplies, drawing farm equipment, rounding up cattle, dragging logs from the forest—the horse was a worker in early British Columbia. It was no easy life. Almost every account of nineteenth century travels records horses plunging to their deaths in canyons or collapsing, exhausted, in deep mud. 'British Columbia is truly a horse-killing country,' notes one observer. Mules and oxen worked as draught animals as well, but the horse was predominant. In time, of course, the horse's role diminished. The internal combustion engine became the source of power for transportation, farming and logging. Some people, though, never abandoned the horse as motive power. Bill Hampton's father and grandfather used horses, just as he does today on his Fraser Valley farm. Shown above fertilizing his fields by means of a horse-drawn manure spreader, Hampton does as much of his farm work as possible using his teams of horses. He is one of a growing number of farmers and independent loggers who are making draught horses once more part of the British Columbia scene.

SHOEING MULES—Just west of Quesnel, in Cariboo country, lies a farm with what seems at first an odd assortment of animals and machinery. But when you note that it's called Heritage Farm, and that owner Milton Swanson is a farrier, blacksmith and old-time fiddler, things begin to make sense. Swanson is entranced by the old ways, and keeps the heritage alive by collecting old farm machinery, honing old skills, and making use of animals most people see only in picture books. He raises Norwegian fjord horses and mules, is on call to shoe draught animals within an 80-kilometre radius of his home, runs an old-fashioned blacksmith's forge, and still finds time to practice up on jigs, reels and waltzes for old-time fiddlers' contests. Shown here shoeing a mule at Cottonwood House, Swanson is doing all he can to keep British Columbia's farming heritage alive.

HORSE LOGGING NEAR QUESNEL—Don McIntosh never really said goodbye to draught animals. When he was eight years old and living in Manitoba, he drove a mule team that 'had forgotten more than I ever knew.' For a number of years, he rambled around in logging and commercial fishing, then settled down on a Cariboo ranch, where he got involved with draught horses—breeding them, breaking them, selling them, loving them. 'I've never seen a tractor yet you could pat on the head and it would nuzzle you back,' he notes. 'All the years I worked with tractors, I never saw a baby tractor.' McIntosh has moved on now, but the horses he bred and sold work the farms and small logging operations of several dozen converts to horsepower. Some use their horses mainly for logging, hearkening back to the days when almost every tree cut in B.C. was hauled to the mill by horses. Most have small farms, where they find using horses more economical and more efficient than using engine power. Across British Columbia and especially in the Cariboo, a network of the owners of draught horses has grown up, to talk, trade information, and organize and compete in horse shows.

Blossom, Fraser Valley

Irving House, New Westminster

Long Beach, Vancouver Island